# Demystifying
## Business
# Cases

For Information Technology, GIS and more....

# Greg J. Duffy MBA

Copyright © 2013 Greg J. Duffy

ISBN:
978-0-9920021-0-7

## *DEDICATION*

I am deeply indebted to my friends and co-workers on the Exchange Planning team at Bell Canada in Toronto twenty-five years ago. That was when Warren Waithe first introduced me to creating telephone exchange area maps on a computer screen using AutoCAD software. He dazzled me by being able to save the work and then redraw it next time the file was opened for a needed change; in only minutes.

WOW. How powerful was that?

Our co-workers Sharon Bray, Carrie Brown, Lee Elder, Sandy Hazlett, Debbie Ryckman, Ben Percic and Bruce Won so enthused me to the power of GIS in telecom planning, regulatory enforcement and asset management that I have enjoyed every IT and GIS management assignment in all these intervening years. They proved then that the best process improvement ideas come from those doing the work.

Business cases were much more basic and mostly intuitive; if it looks that good and is that fast it must be beneficial. The value measured was drawing time eliminated. We have come a very long way across the enterprise.

GIS was, is and always will be a fascinating art and science to me in all its applications and variations. GIS has almost unlimited power to inform.

Thanks everyone.

## *ACKNOWLEDGMENTS*

I am truly thankful to my wife and my three successful children who not only commented on earlier drafts but were able to contribute ideas from their own career experiences outside of IT and GIS. A book such as this also needs to be read by professionals who are experienced in dealing with the art and science of proposing Business Cases in a variety of organizations. I appreciated greatly the time taken and the insight given by a number of IT-GIS friends who read various earlier versions of this book. Among these friends were Don Armstrong, Dan Bowditch, Rob Carroll, Pierre Dupras, Armando LaCivita, Mike MacLean, John Marshall, Kris Philpott and Chris Wilkinson. Each are successful Information and Technology practitioners and advisors in their own right. Everyone gave useful and actionable feedback along with very welcome encouragement.

# Contents

# PROLOGUE

Demystify the process and make your business case defensible, highly effective or even bulletproof. That is a very strong concept. One supposes that no case or presentation is truly bulletproof if the shooter is powerful enough (or unreasonable enough) and the targets are near enough. But our point is that we can always try to prevent being a target, a victim, or a casualty to arbitrary or biased critics. Big shots at close range too often get away with it for lack of a strong defense. This book is designed to help you protect your technology business case and sometimes yourself from naysayers and other random shooters. After all, this is actually in the best interests of the organization. Worthy business cases that support the business, employees and customers, should be defensible in their own right, they should survive arbitrary attacks from target shooters and shotgun style managers.

Demystify! Early on we were going to title this book for writing a *Defensible* business case. We also toyed with the terms of *highly effective* and *compelling* but they too were not good enough on their own. This was because we think that your business case for IT can not only be defended, is defensible, but that the document itself can defend the case without super salesman human presentation. That's also bulletproof, highly effective and compelling! The idea of writing a case document that is self explanatory, self-defending and self promoting is core to our RVI best practice approach. By RVI, as you will learn, we include dollar **Returns**, near-dollar strategic and goodwill **Values** plus **Impacts** on employees or customers/citizens.

We settled on demystify because we were writing not as much about the case but about writing and reading and judging the case. That is what needed to be demystified. It's as much about the people involved as about the text in the story. It is about technique and nuance as much as content.

Too many business cases in Geospatial Information Technologies (GIT, Geo-IT) and in all branches of IT get super favorable reviews because some sales teams are smoother, happier and much more optimistic than perhaps the case warrants. Unfortunately, even though Geographic Information Systems (GIS) are all about data, too often the colorful map impresses when the intelligence of the pattern, the located intelligence, is what should really excite. So lower caliber and possibly overly costly, or out of sequence projects, succeed where they should not.

The merits of the case should be obvious in the supporting document. The document should be defensible, bulletproof, in its own right, without needing excessive salesmanship.   Internal marketing and promotion is always useful but best done to educate your audiences, your reviewers and to do so with best info not best hype.

Unfortunately, really worthwhile projects of all sizes get shot down by individuals or committees that focus their aim on certain parts of the case. This creates the doubt that is shared, sometimes loudly. The math or the operational processes are all too often misunderstood. Sometimes the eventual application cannot be envisioned in the new time and space. Too often the case is attacked by rhetorical questions about the source of supporting data, the accuracy or timeliness of facts and opinions.

As well, questions are raised about how or where or who or when employees, customers or partners will benefit. Some can't bring themselves to align with the overall goal. Some protest that they haven't been given the right defensible story: honestly and tactfully, realistically and sincerely. What they only want to understand is:

- What is the problem or opportunity in the current or approaching time
- What is the impact of this current state on the corporation or a department
- What are peers and competitors doing about similar situations
- What three choices are available to be presented in the business case

Many cases that are denied are often very good viable projects that would actually have brought positive results in a reasonable time. Regrettably, they fail approval because the executive approvers don't *see* the problem, don't *understand* the processes, are unable to *calculate* the implications/risks of approval or denial. They are therefore unable to *envision* the new state that results from a timely execution of the proposed project. Sometimes there just isn't enough money. Lack of money does not make a strong defensible bulletproof business case a failure; it only makes it unfunded ... for a time.

Let's be realistic here. Good and conscientious employees do not submit poor ideas on purpose. Maybe their written words, their business case documents themselves, kill the concept because they did not have a coach to help them tell the story effectively.

We all know that every successful project needs an executive champion. On the other hand we also need to understand that potentially successful projects must not readily succumb to managerial skeptics and attackers. The merits of the case, well presented, should overcome habitual skeptics, naysayers and devil's advocates. You likely know who these people are in your organization by their reputation.

So while bulletproof may seem ambitious if really big guns insist on pre-loading their opinions and biases, the defensible business case should survive. Such cases should be kept at hand, on the list, until funds are available or until the forecasted day arrives. We suggest that all business cases be kept in a pending file even if they fail to be funded in their proposal year. One never knows when the urgency will become major, the funding becomes available or a third factor will raise the critical value of the proposal. In other words, don't throw them out if they fail the funding threshold in a year or a few years. Perhaps review them every year to re-test their applicability.

One of our overarching themes in writing this book and in others to come is what we call RVI™ or Returns, Values and Impacts. In our view it is very important and really very effective to be sure that all technology investments are measured in terms of the financial monetary Returns generated, the non-financial or near-financial Values built in the corporation's capacity and capabilities as well as gauging the Impacts that the investment will have on how many employees, customers or prospects.

# RVI: our Returns, Values, Impacts model for I&T management

We sincerely hope you enjoy reading this book and benefit from its content. After you use what you have learned by reading this book, we ask you to measure us by Returns, Values and Impacts (RVI™):

- ➢ Returns:
    - o Did the acquired knowledge from this book save review time or achieve more consent (or less dissent) more efficiently when writing and presenting your recent business case?
    - o Did you save time and expense on a business case prep after you read this book
    - o Was there a return on your improved knowledge investment?
- ➢ Values:
    - o By using the newly acquired knowledge and skills, did you add value to the corporation's business case processes, to the capacity of your firm or the capabilities of your team?
    - o Did you earn value from reading this book, are you a better employee for having read it and applied its concepts?
- ➢ Impacts:
    - o Did you positively impact the REVIEWERS of your case document or the overseers of the process?
    - o Did this book impact you as a person, as an employee or as a business case stakeholder?

## Suggestions for Reading this Book

We suggest that you quickly read through this book once to get the overall sense and approach that we are sharing with you. Then, in a few days, read it through again and make notes. Make lists of costs, benefits, revenues et cetera by department or function, process or key performance indicator (KPI). Use spreadsheets if necessary, keeping in mind the acquired knowledge from the book's last Section "The Demystified I&T GIS Business Case Companion Financial Workbook". While many of the points covered in this book will make sense on reading, some will only sink in after careful thought and application on a case that is close to you.

You may wish to design your own spreadsheets, utilize corporate templates or purchase a set in our IT Business Case Companion Financial Workbook. For each reading, try to mentally refer to a GIS or other IT project with which you are familiar; whether it is small, medium or large. For a second or third reading, fill out the cells on worksheets (by subject) in as much detail as you can without spending too much time and effort in actual research. Save researching specifics for a real case.

Once you have comfortably defined the outline of your target business case, you should go back and actually conduct a detailed Return on Investment review. Be careful to use each worksheet in the specified order and fill in as many pieces of information as possible. With these spreadsheet templates, it is better to research the details (granularity) and get data to improve the precision, defensibility and marketability of the case. Remember that the case document should ideally be such a well-told story that it sells itself, that secondary presentations and arguments are not needed. Numbers are there to strengthen and support the narrative and to outline a sense of size and scale.

By understanding these basic approaches to Information and Technology (I&T) business cases and the valuation techniques for I&T investments, you will be able to find the necessary input costs, benefits and values while keeping to the 80/20 approach for the project scope. By using multiple categories and types of costs, savings and benefits, the case story will speak to the diligence and the rigor of your research. That in turn makes your recommendation much more solid and clearly more compelling.

Your mission, if you choose to accept it, is not impossible. It is merely for you to describe an opportunity to resolve a problem using an I&T solution as a direct cure or as a mitigation plan. Alternatively, your I&T solution may even be positioned as a support tool for a parallel operational or organizational cure. Your story about the problem and your compelling Preferred Plan must be in sync. Your solution must target the problem and cure it, at least 80% of it.

The narrative of the business case must be written so as to defend itself. The numbers are instrumental in supporting the story, but they are not the story itself. Numbers reflect the troublesome outcomes of the current problem versus the beneficial outcomes resulting from the proposed solution. There is one gripping story that describes the problem's outcomes and a sequel story that describes the solution's outcomes. Clearly told will be clearly understood.

We have inserted two types of alerts in various sections of the book for your added awareness.

The ***Take Note*** inserts offer opportunities to put the book down for a short while and do an assignment, homework if you like. You may find you wish to follow our suggestion or you may prefer to simply think about the idea for a few minutes before continuing your reading. This is your choice.

The **_Geo-IDEA_** inserts emphasize how GIS and other geospatial applications and processes can be referenced or researched when learning to write effective bullet-proof business cases involving information and technology. Geo-IDEA is meant to convey a number of themes you may wish to use in your geo-case writing:

**I** implies INNOVATIVE: or perhaps Information or Improve or Investment; to help you think about your corporate and user personality or persona as web designers like to call it

**D** implies DISTINCTIVE: or perhaps Direct or Direction or Disseminate or Disclose; to enable you to get their attention

**E** implies EFFECTIVE: or perhaps Enterprise or Enabling or Efficient; so your audiences can envisage a new normal

**A** implies ACCELERATIVE: or perhaps Applications or Awareness or Availability or Access: to add to the mission of "let's do it".

# INTRODUCTION

Wikipedia (Feb 2013) identifies "The **first law of geography** according to Waldo Tobler in 1970"as:

- "Everything is related to everything else, but near things are more related than distant things."
- "This observation is embedded in the gravity model of trip distribution. It is also related to the law of demand, in that interactions between places are inversely proportional to the cost of travel between them"

So we embark on discussing how GIS/IT business cases help organizations describe and justify investments in geo-information (or geospatial) based technologies and processes so as to manage their connecting and interacting of everything that is related to something else in their business. Most readers understand the basics of GIS, that things/people are at points on the earth, that lines of roads, wires or rivers often connect them to each other. We intuitively understand clusters of like-minded people living in houses on streets within areas of various government, business or ad hoc areas.

**Points**, **lines** and **polygons** are the world's most fascinating and fun connect-the-dots game whether by town, county, census tract, serving area or trade area. Most business people now accept that well over 80% of all business matters relate to location, to "where" the asset is, the transaction occurs or as Mr. Tobler said, to what is nearby. Indeed some say that this concept of awareness or better still, *a-where-ness*, has become fundamental to our understanding of almost everything in life and business.

Investments are made in Information and Technology (I&T or I/T or just IT) in order to improve the ability of an organization to become more efficient or more effective and therefore to survive, prosper and grow. Connecting services to customers, inputs to products and employees to work activities is basic to GIS/IT tools and applications.

Such investments are made in the expectation of maintaining or increasing an organization's ability to add capacity and capability to its infrastructure, its physical resources and its human resources. Motives include corporate survival, competitive success and even increased fame or market presence. Generally the challenge of 'growing' an organization to add capacity or capability is found between the extremes of "build it and they will come" and "all our peers are doing this" on the *why shouldn't we* side all the way over to "we can't afford to invest at this time" and "we can't while we fight for survival" of the *why should we* side.

Adding information *and* technology (note the '*and*') means that we add data to our repository, then add hardware/communications to connect people to our data, and then add software to help people use the data they access. The result is that the information, intelligence and wisdom which derive from the I&T project becomes accessible and usable by employees or customers. That is what delivers value through the added capacity and capability.

A singular best practice benefit from GIS that has intrigued us for so many years is its ability to enable visualization. GIS can help the viewer 'see', and then understand, business performance and process patterns. As importantly, GIS can overcome anecdotal visions of patterns that in fact are not present or are misleadingly wrong. Your bullet-proof business case story can enable your audiences to visualize your suggested outcomes, both on screen and more importantly, in their own minds. Once they can 'see' how your project will turn out in terms of key performance patterns, they can accept their way to approve funding. Be sure to use GIS as part of your business case proof of concept if you can. Walk the talk.

This book delivers a practical overview guide for what is involved in determining the value of a proposed investment project in I&T systems from the desktop to the enterprise, whether internally focused or outwardly putting information and services on the web.

This guide is written for what we call REVIEWERS who are executives, managers, team leaders, team members, employees in general (and students of business) and those who may have direct, indirect, formal or informal responsibility for writing, reviewing or approving business cases; any and all stakeholders and observers in fact. It is written in a manner to coach those non-financial employees who find themselves faced with financial ratios such as Return on Investment (ROI), IRR (Internal Rate of Return) and Net Present Value (NPV) and Pay Back period (PB).

This guide is specifically not written for expert accounting and finance managers as their needs are more specific to their professions and training. This guide is for those involved with the problem or the opportunity at hand:

- Those who may propose or present an investment solution;
- Those who may inherit the investment's end product or application;

- Those who are operational decision makers and project sponsors;
- Those who lead and govern the IT, the operating Division or the enterprise;

Our goal is to help the staff or line Manager or Director, the business unit leaders or I&T unit directors and managers assess the general wisdom of a recommended technology investment. Part of the story speaks to the estimated costs, benefits and returns of an investment in Data or Information, Hardware or Communications, out-of-the-box Software or configured Applications. A business case becomes a well presented blend of context, history, data and strategy woven in a manner that is readily understood by all stakeholders.

Decision makers at all levels need the best available and most current information on which to base their decisions. Senior management boards and governance bodies need to be assured that all investments are documented, scrutinized, evaluated, justified and shared openly. Only then can project approval decisions properly be made well, transparently, and with rigorous consistent processes delivered in advance to permit thoughtful investigation and comment.

Most organizations find it useful and convenient for all business cases and project justifications to be developed using consistent approaches, basic templates and standard questions. It is in fact usually required. With consistent documentation and format methods, it leaves only the merits of the case, the need to satisfy the business drivers, as the prime influencer for the investment. This book and an XLS workbook will enable you to standardize your approach and level the playing field for GIS/IT project evaluation at the introduction stage, the planning stage when the issue first arises and first undergoes formulation and some escalation.

Poorly written documents no matter how officially formatted will (and should) fail to adequately make the case. Executives should never approve poorly presented cases, even when they fully support the project. These executives should look ahead with some concern to audits, public and press feedback, regulatory oversight and any other review post-project that asks "who approved this?" or "why did they ever approve that case?". But projects should not be cancelled or shot down simply out of such fear or concern, should they? Each approved case should have clearly documented benefits and rationale.

Well written documents will enlighten all stakeholders about the nature of the problem, the nature of the solution, the business context of the strategy, the best expectations of financial matters and the clarity of the preferred decision. With that in their possession, all stakeholders, reviewers and authorities will rest easy about future feedback. As a case writer you hope for the day the CEO, CFO or CIO says something like "why can't all IT business cases be as clear and compelling as this one?"

Speaking practically, decision makers need to determine:

- which GIS or I&T projects get approved:
  - the go versus no-go choice,
- which GIS or I&T projects get deferred:
  - the now versus later choice and
- which solution gets modified:

- o the optimal versus sub-optimal choice or
- o the full scope versus phased approach choice.

The numbers and the dollars will support the compelling business story and provide a way for senior managers to rank or compare various project proposals. That is why one needs to know these ratios, the ROI and NPV at least. But the key challenge is the narrative, the story, told in such a way that enables all readers to understand and to select appropriate actions within their own job scope or new comfort level.

The ideas, concepts and lessons of this book should be accompanied by financial and activity based spreadsheets such as MS Excel Workbooks. These would be formatted and geared to capturing the essential work activities, monies and other values that the Business Case needs in order to be worthy of approval, to make its case.

We sincerely hope you find this guide helpful, easy to read and easy to adapt to your particular need. We expect that you will be able to obtain the inputs (dollars, hours, work units etc.) from the business units. We trust your executives will appreciate your ability to present a balanced business case which includes these financial style ratios along with a compelling narrative, one which balances dollar based returns with structural value and aligns with the corporate mission, answering 'why' you are in business in the first place.

While reading this book we suggest you think about a business project, a technology one preferably and perhaps a GIS/geospatial application if you know of one. By keeping such a project in mind you may find it much easier to apply the thoughts and suggestions we are offering you.

Use the suggested **_'Take Note'_** actions, sort of like an assignment or homework, so that you make reading the book more immediately useful to you, more relevant to business matters with which you may be familiar.  While the points covered will make sense on reading, they will only sink in after some thought and application on a case matter you know about.

# BUSINESS CASE BASICS

## Business Cases versus Business Plans

According to Wikipedia (March 2013):

"A **Business Case** captures the reasoning for initiating a project or task. It is often presented in a well-structured written document, but may also sometimes come in the form of a short verbal argument or presentation…in support of a business need. An example could be that (while) a software upgrade might improve system performance …the "business case" (value) is that better performance would improve customer satisfaction, require less task processing time, or reduce system maintenance costs. A compelling business case adequately captures both the quantifiable and unquantifiable characteristics of a proposed project."

"Consideration should also be given to the option of doing nothing; including the costs and risks of inactivity. From this information, the justification for the project is derived. Note that it is not the job of the project manager to build the business case (as) this task is usually the responsibility of stakeholders and sponsors."

and

"A **Business Plan** is a formal statement of a set of business goals, the reasons they are believed attainable, and the plan for reaching those goals. It may also contain background information about the organization or team attempting to reach those goals. Business plans may also target changes in perception and branding by the customer, client, taxpayer, or larger community. When the existing business is to assume a major change or when planning a new venture, a 3 to 5 year business plan is required, since investors will look for their annual return in that timeframe."

So, **Business Plans** are about the whole business entity or a major division while **Business Cases** are about single projects typically in individual business units. Remember that a project by definition has:

- a **start** or beginning based on approval, funding, resource allocation and staffing
- a **delivery** or execution period during which resources are merged to create a process or output defined in the project's set of deliverables
- and an **end**, a completion of all work followed by closure of the project accounts
- and then followed by an audit, check-up or look-back of some degree to decide if the project objectives were in fact met e.g. to answer at least the 'on-time', 'on-budget', 'on-scope' questions ... where possible given parallel changes over time.

Business Cases compete against each other through budget cycles usually managed by a Portfolio Management Office (PMO) in the I&T or Finance department. Business cases would expect, if approved and funded, to begin within one or two years, run two to three years in execution and finish completely within five years.

Business Plans are more typically strategic in nature but with tactical goals at certain time intervals. Business Plans represent intentions and indications of how to achieve them. Business Cases describe individual strategically tactical steps that need to be taken to solve a problem or exploit an opportunity to improve processes so as to reach better performance levels that align with overall corporate key indicators and goals. The completions of business cases that fulfill the intentions of a business plan are common.

A set of related projects with a common or complementary end description can be grouped into a Program. The sum of all Projects and Programs becomes the Portfolio for the I&T division. The PMO (project management office or portfolio management office) controls the Portfolio. The term PPM of Project Portfolio Management is gaining in popularity.

## TIP: The author of the business case is responsible for getting the approvers to understand... before one can ever hope to get them to approve.

Remember that when you publish your written case, you have become the best expert in the entire organization with regard to this unique subject. Be confident in your knowledge and take all advice under consideration. Give credit to your contributors. While many of your peers may better understand their own particular part, you best understand the sum of the parts as well as each part. You are good, really good, a definite asset so present your case with strength and sincerity. Some who take shots at you may have their own agenda so don't let that distract you from knowing your case, its strengths and its importance.

The best technologies are robust and resilient; agile and lean.

So are the most compelling defensible bullet-proof business cases.

So are the best highly effective case writers.

## Business Cases tell a Story

### *Think "I have a dream": not "Once-upon-a-time"!*

A Business Case is essentially a story. Ideally it is a very a compelling story, about a business problem or an opportunity for which the recommended solution includes an I&T investment. It is predominantly a narrative. In the Prologue above we identified that approval committees and empowered individuals too often fail to see and understand the today scenario and then the tomorrow scenario. They just don't get it. They don't get into the story. It is not their fault. The author of the business case is the only one responsible for getting the approvers to understand, to be in the picture and to ultimately align with the project.

So writing and telling the story, as a story, an imaginable scenario of cause and effect, of a here-we-are today and a what-about tomorrow is how you enable them to have a part in your project. A number of advisors today who coach on how to improve speeches, papers and presentations (with or without PowerPoint) are urging us to deliver our talk like a story. They emphasize that audiences are much more able to understand and participate in a story describing actions in and actions out. It really is that simple.

Interestingly, Michael Selzner (socialmediaexaminer.com) recalls interviewing author Dave Kerpen (Likeable Social Media) and says that:

- "Dave believes that telling their story showed …that it's not about understanding the tools, it's about understanding how to be creative and think outside the box" and

- "by being able to tell a story, you're able to bring some real personality to what it is you do, and at the same time, convince people that you know what you are doing," and
- "whether you are at a boardroom ... or pitching to a prospect ...story telling can bring your business (case) alive. It can help you connect with your audience (readers). And it can eventually persuade people."

One wonders how many technology business cases never gain momentum because the audience doesn't really understand the play unfolding in the context of their business operations. They don't 'imagine' the story of the problem themselves or they don't respect the expertise of the author, the business case presenter? Too many no doubt.

## *Defining and Knowing Your Audiences*

In order to properly face any of your audiences you need to understand that members have varying histories. Every person, manager, team, board and council is made up of people who may or may not be knowledgeable and may or may not be sufficiently objective. Simply said you need to find out who is a member of each audience and find ways to appeal to their particular needs or biases. We all have biases. You need to address their business issues related to your case and be able to alert them to the basic premise and basic value of your case...as it pertains to their role in the enterprise. Again, that is why the story approach is so effective.

For some audiences you may meet them on the elevator or in a lunch line. Others you may actually report to and others you may never have met or even know about. It is the job of the case writer to find out as much as possible about each member of each audience. That way you can better research and write about your project from their eyes and to their ears.

The most basic qualities of successful sale people is their ability to "overcome objections". That is also a major requirement in selling your business case. Lucky for you there are opportunities to head off objections by dealing with your audience members well before they actually sit in judgment.

Why? Well, not so that you can just try to sell them on your case and your project. It is so you can be sure that their interests are dealt with in your case. If the audience member is involved with the user community make certain to deal with all user issues and opportunities. If the costs and financial benefits interest them, be sure to cover all aspects of the money side and any material matters regarding financial ratios and expectations. If they are interested in regulatory, public affairs or board governance be sure to cover those aspects. And so on …

A really good reason to adopt a story telling approach is that every audience member, yes every one of them, does not have anywhere near the knowledge about the issue and the solution that you do. You must educate them, and you must do that *before* they are asked to approve your case. If you write a document that is too technical you will lose half of the audience. Or worse they will be unduly influenced by the tech types who may overpower your presentation. On the other hand if you describe the story of what happens now, who does what and the outcomes that occur, everyone will have the same understanding as each other. It is very hard to take random or targeted shots at a case document when your peers in that audience are equally armed. There is little advantage to being a shooter. You level the playing field when you tell the current story. You really make the decision process more even when you tell the 'after' story based on a shared equal understanding of the before story at the same time.

You should also consider audience attitude, objectivity, style and maybe even their tolerance for matters that they really do not understand or care much about. This is mostly about their psychology, style, background, ability, rank and awareness of broad business issue affecting the organization. While it may be impossible to fully prepare for this aspect of audience awareness you might find it useful to read all or parts of a number of current books about how people think and how people approach decisions.

Among those known to us are:

- Thinking Fast, and Slow by Dr. Daniel Kahneman who speaks to how people have two thinking styles, System One and System Two.
- Why Great Leaders Don't Take Yes for an Answer, by Dr. Michael Roberto; and Know What You Don't Know (How Great Leaders Prevent Problems Before They Happen).
- A number of publications and white papers from CIMA, the Chartered Institute of Management Accountants (in UK) speak to VBM or Value Base Management and in varying detail speaks to the applicability of ratios such as ROI, IRR and NPV.
- Systems providers such as IBM, Pink Elephant, ESRI, Intergraph and others have published a wide variety of white papers on subjects relevant to the financial ratios and their applicability in IT, GIS and business intelligence in general.
- Leading consultancies such as Gartner Group, Boston Consulting, KPMG and Deloitte among many others have published a wide variety of white papers on subjects relevant to the financial ratios and their applicability.
- And many more if you Google or Bing creatively.

As a technique for writing a business case, if you take a position on how you calculated or why you chose certain input factors you may find it highly worthwhile to be able to refer to published comments whose guidance you followed. You can be sure that at least one leading reviewer in each of your audiences will have their own view with which you may have to duel. Be well armed and bring backup.

***Take Note***:    For a recent I&T project you are knowledgeable about can you imagine or even write a short description that explains how a story method was or would have been an ideal way to sell that project? Can you think about whether the marketing of that project was or would have been easier when the story approach is the key delivery vehicle?

## The Business Case REVIEWERS.

For those who like acronyms, and who in I&T doesn't, we offer a summary here of the members of your various business case audiences. Easy to remember perhaps.

R.E.V.I.E.W.E.R.S are:
- ***Readers***: those who are expected to read your case narrative or presentation slides out of personal or departmental interest (or because you asked them to check it) and who report questions, suggestions and problems to you. They are very helpful so use them a lot. All actionable feedback is good, keep that thought working for you.
- ***End***-users: The end-users are familiar to us all as those employees or customers or even business partners who currently use the system and who will be the direct users of the new systems. These who are the ones whose current

pain we are trying to resolve with our business case. Their input and support is critical.

- *Visionaries*: those who see even greater good coming after this project completes and they envision add-ons or even brighter opportunities for the enterprise once the problem at hand is cured. Peripheral perhaps but key to marketing your case as a strategic leap forward to a better and healthier company. These are important people because they assume right off that your case is correct and that you will succeed. They want to be there in that strategically better world you are describing.
- *Implementers*:  those who are systems or hardware or data conversion employees or contractors or vendors whose interest in your case has much to do with work they anticipate they will end up doing. Your cure won't work well if poorly executed so keep these implementers on side. They need to be sure you considered their needs, parallel or tangential needs maybe, in your research on costs, resources, deliverables and time and the big one, change management.
- *Employees:* These are the co-workers of end-users, those who work separately from those involved in the processes addressed in your case but who still have an interest in your project's success. Perhaps the call centre staff or field workers who receive complaints from customers. Maybe they envision your new story where these customers will no longer need to complain because the new process or web site or whatever will address them directly and effectively.
- *Writers*: Well that's probably you and your closest associates. You do the research and you do the interviews, the questionnaires, the basic math and the strategic reviews. You do the marketing and the presentations to individuals and groups.
- *Executives*: those whose role is one of oversight and governance, those who are ultimately responsible for the overall direction and success of everything. These people need to be kept informed of your progress and your end goal. They need to be 'on-side' long before the critical decision making meeting. You should meet individually with

each of these people (or their most trusted advisor) when major projects are being proposed.

- *Regulators*: those in government generally or regulation enforcement specifically who will see your project as beneficial to their role. It may affect compliance of some sort, or just reporting or maybe even investigating. The regulator may be formal like an energy commission or informal like an elected official who takes it upon himself to act as a regulation monitor.

- *Stakeholders*: those who are 'a person, group or organization with an interest in a project' (Wikipedia March 2013). In fact just about everyone else who wants to know about your project and the results of its implementation and completion. Stakeholders can be individuals, groups, organizations or people who will be affected if the project succeeds (e.g. the new web site) or fails to proceed (e.g. the open data initiative from the GIS division).

# Intro to Nine Steps to Effective Business Cases

In order to set a base upon which to read the rest of this book and more importantly to start your business case writing career we offer the following a nine step model for a standard IT and/or GIS Business Case. Please note that the number nine is not fixed, it simply represents one easy way to divide the work of researching and writing your case. Longer is not considered better. Only well written, concise, to the point, covering all important aspects honestly and completely is better.

While a number of organizations have template driven 'standard' models and frameworks from which they expect I&T and other Business Cases to be written, there really are only nine best practice sections that each must have. We emphasize starting with the elevator pitch, the short summary of the proposed project itself. Nine easy steps. Keep it simple. The Neat Nine if you like. Break each of the nine into sub-parts if you insist, but make sure you research, test and write to complete each of these sections. These are the 'must haves' of all business cases for all business investments, not just IT and not just GIS.

Keep in mind as you digest this sequence that your business case, your published one, would likely be less than 50 pages, more likely 30 to 40. You may include an appendix of some key insightful *summary* graphs, tables, lists, surveys and diagrams but you would not expect too many stakeholders to actually attempt to read or understand them. No doubt you would also have hundreds of emails on file, a drawer or two of paper files and maybe even a number of vendor brochures, peer reviews and media articles filed somewhere digitally or in paper. Back-up is for proving your research and diligence and for being summarized in your business case narrative.

Back-up is just back-up, not content. It does not become part of a 75-200 page binder that will shock and scare your stakeholders.

So until the more detailed Nine Step Model discussion in Section 5, here are the basic steps you will learn about by reading this book. Keep these steps in mind as you read through.

For our nine  steps we have created a triangular grouping of the nine parts as shown.

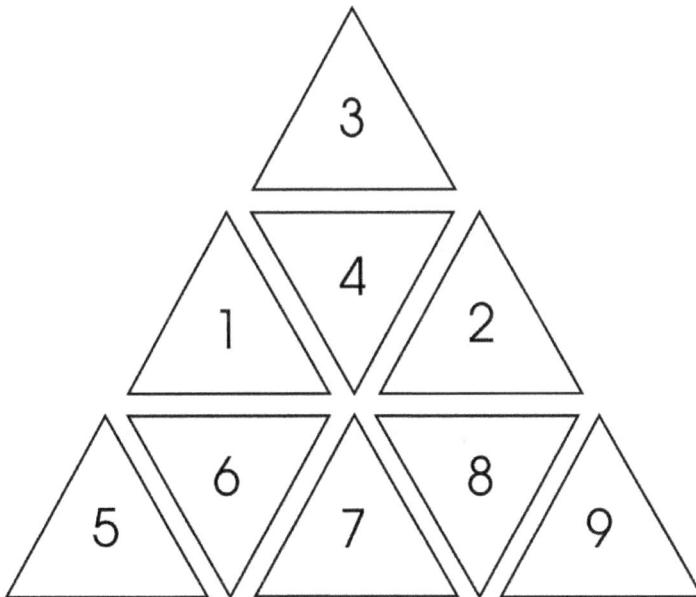

As you will understand in Section 5 we feel one would start with the description of the problem or opportunity that was brought to the case writer's attention, Step 3 below. That is why we place that at the top starting point. You may choose to start your own documentation wherever you felt most comfortable, even if you readily saw a solution and were quite comfortable with writing about that first and working backwards, taking care to stay narrowly focused on the problem.

While good case documents can be written from back to front you must be very careful not to be so fond of the solution that you fail to prove the problem. I&T has had too many solutions looking for problems to solve over the years and that has hurt many reputations among users, analysts and of course vendors.

Normally we divide the nine steps into three sets of three.

The first being the start of the Elevator Pitch and the broadest outline of the intro to the Executive Summary both based on the details of the current problem or opportunity of the Current Situation.

## The Elevator Pitch, the Current Situation and Executive Summary

| 1 | Elevator Pitch | • A 20-40 word 15-25 second summary of the problem, the pain and the likely cure formulated up front to share with eventual stakeholders that sets out an initial scope for your business case narrative<br>• This pitch becomes a presentation title, a meeting agenda topic, when your case is finished and you are marketing it throughout your organization |
|---|---|---|
| 2 | Executive Summary | • The Executive Summary is written last because only then do you know what to say, only then can you expand your pitch by taking key text from every section, in order, throughout your now 30-40 page report.<br>• This summary is meant to be one page, just one page, because we expect senior managers and approvers to only read one page, to understand from one page |
| 3 | Current Situation | • This is a well told story describing in some detail the current situation in which a problem or opportunity has been identified and an IT/GIS cure is anticipated<br>• This section includes details of why the current situation is a problem, who and what processes are affected and which costs, penalties, service levels and even reputations are in trouble because of this problem or missed opportunity.<br>• Identify which division or person 'owns' this problem |

The second phase takes the writer into the details of the Current Costs, the resultant Rationale for Action and the identification of the Top Three Options as it flows from the first phase of the current issue.

## Current Costs; Rationale for Action; the Top Three Options

| 4 | Effects Costs and Risks of Current Situation | • In this section we determine the service, financial and image costs that the current problem is triggering.<br>• We get a sense of the risks, penalties and adverse impacts of the problem and our readers begin to feel the pain<br>• Whomever owns the problem is calling for a cure |
|---|---|---|
| 5 | Rationale for Action | • This speaks to why action is necessary or valuable and speaks to corporate image, risk mitigation, service levels and growth indicators, cost management, KPIs<br>• This is where we can look at peers, industry practices to begin creating a 'view' of a better corporate world for us and our organization. |
| 6 | Top Three Options to Consider | • Here we delve into the top three options, the only three presentable options.<br>• Here we begin to enlighten our audience on which option may likely be preferred and why, not because we tell them but because they see it coming, they see the intuitive advantages arising for one of the options |

The third phase of our research and writing works on Weighing the Options, making Recommendations and outlining Resources required to go forward as it builds logically on the flow from the second part.

## Weighing options, the Recommendation and Resource needs

| 7 | Returns Values and Impacts of Each Option | <ul><li>Each option is detailed in terms of costs, benefits, regulations, risks, methods, resources, timing, market support to generate Returns</li><li>Explain each option's strategic Value with a slight emphasis on the improvements the stronger option may have in Impacting employees, customers or other stakeholders</li><li>Discuss the stronger option, the now preferred option, last so that the reader retains this in mind</li></ul> |
|---|---|---|
| 8 | Recommendation and Rationale | <ul><li>Drive home the reasons for the preferred option and why it is recommended at this time</li><li>This is the conclusion of the comparative section but one expects the audience to already understand why the preferred option is the best one. If this section is still weak it is only because the prior two sections were not clear.</li><li>This is where one identifies measurements that may be revealed after the project.</li><li>Most REVIEWERS love to measure outcomes</li></ul> |
| 9 | Project Outline and Resource Expectations | <ul><li>Before any committee or person will approve and fund your project you must outline a general schedule of high level project plans plus a sense of resources and money that will be needed by when for what</li><li>This is not a project level plan but a calendar level quarterly outline of what needs to be planned in detail following approval to proceed.</li></ul> |

## **Appendices and Exhibits**

An appendix is not back-up. An appendix is a minimal number of pieces of confirmation or evidence of acceptability (credibility if you prefer) for important statements or themes noted in your case narrative. In that sense it is part of your brief, your case. Be sure to not add something in the appendix which was not addressed specifically in the case documented story.

Examples of appendix material might be a list of every contributor to the case document. This may be very useful for the obvious reason of thanking them for helping but also for the critical survival issue of ensuring their bosses know that they contributed and that some serious amount of content in the business case came from inside their own division (hopefully with much credibility).

Your appendix is merely a reasonable number of tables, charts, lists and graphics that follow and directly support any of your nine key parts. You may also include a bibliography of sources where copyright or appreciation is acknowledged.

# BUSINESS CASES & INVESTMENT RETURNS

## What Are IT/GIS Investments Supposed to Accomplish?

This guide is written for case writers primarily but also very much for executives, directors, business unit managers, I&T managers, business analysts, project team members, strategy managers, consultants and solution providers who are constantly challenged to justify expenditures for information, data and technology. This guide is meant to help authors, reviewers and approvers of I&T Business Cases whose task is to explain, in straightforward understandable words:

- What the core of the investment request is about
- What it will do for the firm's processes and outcomes
- What are the reasons for doing it, why now or later and why in this manner
- What the necessary resource and financing requirements will be
- What need the project fulfills and what it actually buys
- Whether it solves a problem or exploits an opportunity or perhaps both
- What savings it creates or what revenues it triggers
- How it enhances efforts to align with and meet corporate goals/missions and
- What the operational and financial payback will be, when and in what value terms

## TIP: I&T investments should build *capability* in employees and *capacity* in the organization in order to increase the agility of both.

For too long the I&T sector has treated both the 'I' and the 'T' as if they were fused as one subject: just IT. In fact for too long the I&T sector has appeared to favor the tangible, the Technology, the toys. Historically the hardware was a very expensive large share of projects. Today the hardware and software seem more reasonable in simple price levels but also in price per unit of utility. More value seems to be there and competitive pressures keep vendors working hard for your business. So today we need to keep the cost/value balance evenly in our minds for each of the 'I' and the 'T'. If technology is being seen more as a commodity today there is validity in that. Good data, now known to be strategically valuable, a critical asset, is so costly to duplicate and so devastating if compromised.

Good data is not a commodity and never has been.

Good technology is readily available and now more cost effective than ever.

Good software can be expensive but it is now so very dynamic, broadly installed, extensively tested and well understood by user communities who share knowledge and fixes, tips and tricks.

## *Investing in Data and Information*

These investments will enhance the flow of knowledge which delivers intelligence. This in turn enables employees of an organization to work in ways that save money, earn money or improve service. They do this through improved awareness and processes that meet business requirements or enable compliance. Thus they build strategically important confidence and capability in themselves and co-workers that will affect customers or citizens, those for whom the services are destined. When employees know more about a matter before they embark on a work effort, they save time and accomplish better outcomes because they work smarter or more safely. The more they feel they have satisfied their contacts, the less absenteeism and turnover their employer may experience.

***Geo-IDEA:***   *Office based employees can do their work locating problematic incidents or aging assets from digital maps and special imagery (taken from a plane, a satellite or an automobile). This enables them to avoid driving out to inspect or see something. Therefore they save time, need less vehicles, use less fuel and improve productivity. They even lessen the carbon footprint of their work by not emitting unnecessary green-house gases by avoiding field trips or at least making them fewer or much more efficient using improved routing. All of this requires accurate well-maintained data.*

## Investing in Hardware and Communications

These investments will store and deliver the information at the right time to the right person. Investments in these commodity-like tools lead directly to:

- less cost to store data or more data storage capacity per device
- less cost to access data and less cost to transfer data
  - more data per unit of transport
- less personnel cost to access and receive data
- and less building space requiring less electricity for climate control to house the data

For example the lesser use of energy saves money but also contributes directly to lessening the green-house gases and the carbon footprint caused by employees and machines performing their daily work. So for an I&T business case the story becomes more solid as the outcome will positively impact the organization's reputation as well as bringing operating efficiencies.

***GeoIDEA:*** *GIS has always been a large user of I&T infrastructure such as server capacity and communications bandwidth. To avoid this being seen as a negative it is useful to identify the advantages and economies of scale often triggered by adding GIS needs to other corporate needs to get the unit cost down and the data transfer rates up for all data and not just the geodata.*

## Investing in Software and Applications

These investments will facilitate the beneficial use of the data by providing the tools for viewing and understanding the wisdom that the data carries. These investments make the work less error prone, more easily shared and can contribute to facilitating decisions by employees and managers. Organizations will use software thought to be best in class, most effective or most successful depending on the nature of their mission and role. The Business Case effort to identify costs and returns that explain and justify I&T expenditures is the first step in achieving the practices considered as 'best' or 'best in class'.

**TIP: Financial investments in the stock markets of London, New York, Tokyo and Toronto that generate profits and ROI are <u>passive</u> while GIS, BI, CRM, ERP and other I&T investments that build capability and capacity are <u>active</u>. This is a major distinction.**

The value of the returns from I&T investments must be understood before projects get FINALLY approved. Some financial and market based investment ratios such as ROI and NPV have been seen as useful in gaining some understanding about I&T investments and in choosing the priorities. However, the context in which the investment is made, the story behind the need to invest, is the really important part of your analysis. One hears more often recently from commentators, observers, some professional associations and related governance bodies that are suggesting that ROI, on its own, should only represent 20-40% of the decision rationale, the project scoring grid, when business investments are evaluated or planned.

***GeoIDEA:*** *GIS software is normally licensed with the opportunity for annual upgrades as the versions improve based on feedback and demands from a very broad variety of users. It is normally a best practice to agree to the annual incremental updates so as to benefit from new techniques a few at a time. More importantly, annual or regularly scheduled updates avoid your getting behind the marketplace. This in turn avoids having to endure a wholesale major upgrade every few years, with associated change management issues and potentially higher costs. However if you consciously decide to upgrade only on full refresh cycles, you do get the opportunity to evaluate other and competing software platforms or vendors or systems integrators. If so, you need to carefully understand that migrating to a very different platform might be a very expensive time consuming project. Not* *impossible but not to be taken lightly for sure. The main thing is that you clearly indicate the future ongoing costs of options related to the proposed solution.*

**Take Note**: Can you identify a past, current or planned project; maybe a problem or an opportunity not yet explored? For this project, can you list the nature of the capability improvements and/or capacity increases that might be desirable with regard to each of Data/Information, Hardware/Communications and Software/Applications that come to mind?

## *Active Versus Passive Investments*

Market based investments, such as stocks and bonds, are made simply to earn more money, to earn returns directly. These types of direct investments are usually *passive* (e.g. strictly defined, narrowly targeted and specific in expectation and duration). One puts money down, walks away and waits for some brief time, typically two to four years, then cashes out to pocket the gains if there are any. For example one could invest in a 5% bank account or government Treasury Bill that matures in 5 years. Hence a $1000 investment is expected to earn $50 per year times five years or $250 over five years at which point the investment is redeemed for its face value of $1000. The investor sits back passively and waits while his investment earns a return.

I&T investments are *active*. I&T returns are denominated firstly in processes, activities, decisions, and other material activities or outcomes. They are meant specifically to build employee capability and confidence, to increase organizational capacity and to ensure continued agility, robustness of technology and resilience in the GIS/IT resources.

The outcomes of active I&T investments can then be measured in monetary terms, but their base is not money like the interest from a treasury bill. These other investments, such as in BI, ERP, GIS, CRM or other I&T resources, are made to enable a business unit to:

- perform a new process,
- improve an older process,
- do something not previously possible or practicable such as offering new services
- own/buy something which will itself then create more value (such as data) or
- create capacity and capability value, specifically in one business unit or across the organization as a whole.

These investments add capacity and capability because they are active and because they require more context, more time and more real human participation. I&T investments are active because they are dynamic and fluid within broad limits. You put money down to purchase something and you actively use whatever you bought in some business manner to then earn a return. This can sometimes require three to five years or more and, sometimes three to five phases or more.

Investments in DATA or INFORMATION may be reasonably quick to make but will often pay back for a longer time period as they are used repeatedly by more and more applications or people over time as each occasion (e.g. a web-hit) that the data is accessed and used. That's a recurring value.

Investments in HARDWARE technology such as servers may be slower to install and will last only a few short years or will fill to load limits even before their useful life ends.

Investments in SOFTWARE require continuous learning and may need updating with more investment, perhaps even annually by way of maintenance licensing or fixes and patches.

So even though investments in DATA and INFORMATION sometimes seem sizable, their relative added value more than offsets the ongoing investment costs. Data can be a complex acquisition with regard to accuracy, currency, and completeness but the payback is longer as they form an intrinsic portion of the capacity of the organization. This capacity in turn enables increased capability in the hands of employee users or customer site visitors and inquirers. Such added capability usually delivers more confidence for employees in their work activities and more confidence by customers in the company or its products.

Executives have been known to blame high project costs on hardware (vendors notably) and software (conversion consultants typically) more than on data. Perhaps this is understandable and if any room for negotiation exists it would be with hardware and software pricing. But hardware's capacity per dollar is still growing (Moore's Law has long suggested that processing power per dollar doubles every 18 months) and software's many tools continue to grow in usefulness due to feedback from thousands of users. The costs therefore may not actually be so high.

The intrinsic value in more and better data which is more easily accessed and shared is better understood by senior managers who know that good decisions need to come from good information, whether developed, bought or subscribed. An experienced IT or GIS project manager will likely advise you that the major issue is usually the data. Of course that is where the value lies as well. No investment, no projects, no value created. For data, no ongoing investment in quality or timeliness equals errors and equates to losses. Not good.

We recall an IT executive in telecommunications proposing that *'data is a commodity'*. We certainly disagreed by pointing out quite clearly that current, accurate, verified data is actually an asset and when utilized throughout the enterprise on demand, when needed, was a strategic asset, a major differentiator. Attitudes can be very hard to overcome. We hope you don't meet too many such adverse or out of date attitudes.

The Business Case must therefore delineate the value returned from GIS and I&T investments just as much as it needs to capture the costs. GIS and other I&T investments are not the same as financial market investments. That is why we measure I&T investment differently and carefully.

***Take Note***:   Can you identify a small number of generally 'passive' investments your organization might make with its resources? Can you list a bigger number of 'active' investments that could be made to increase/improve a return from its resources?

***Geo-IDEA:***   *The investment of geocoding vast amounts of corporate location based data about assets, transactions, revenues, stores, consumer clusters adds tremendously valuable insight/knowledge (capability) and when these data are accessible they add valuable decision inputs that improve processes (capacity).*

# Numbers, Money and Legal Supports for the Story

Business Cases are usually supported, in numbers and dollars, by estimates of hard or soft costs, benefits (including savings, revenues and cost avoidance) in order to "measure" a return on the investment. Whenever a law, a regulation or an almost compulsory common practice applies, that too supports the story even when numbers or money do not fully indicate desirable investments. Self explanatory spreadsheets and graphs can support the numbers and money aspects of your story. Extracts of regulations and similar proof would support such non-financial or non-volume based stories and projects.

## Hard, Soft and Assigned Costs and Benefit Monies

In all GIS/IT business cases there are what are called *hard* dollars, *soft* dollars and what we often call *assigned* dollar values. These can each be easily identified, quantified and predicted:

- *hard* dollars are those with known prices and fairly fixed units of supply where little variation except quantities can vary the overall project expense
    - These include communications and hardware costs, rent, fuel, full time salaries, parts, interest, taxes, insurance and similar costs
    - Typical expressions of hard costs are $X for 100 notebooks; $Y for 12 new full time equivalent employees; Z% bank interest over three years

- *soft* dollars are those that imply costs and benefits but are often more difficult to quantify with precision or narrow variance
    - These include travel, overtime, training, utilities, wear and tear, depreciation

o   Typical expressions of soft costs are $x increased sales potential per caller per day over two years; y% decrease in overtime in the data centers for off-line maintenance; $z total advertising cost increase over three years

- *assigned values* are very soft dollars which are logically and defensibly imputed as being expected on the project but which cannot be quantified except as broad corporate wide expectations that are assigned to the calculations and noted as to source and rationale
    o   These include revenue gains, sales increases, customer satisfaction indicators, error rates, accidents, inflation, legal liabilities, goodwill etc.
    o   Typical assigned values are along the lines of: a 3-6% increase in general revenues or a 4-7% drop in call centre complaints or a 12-15% improvement in vehicle longevity.
    o   Each of these is logical, anticipated and yet must be assigned a dollar equivalent value as they cannot at the business case stage be proven in fact.
    o   Note that percentage bands are used in the narrative to reinforce the assigned nature of the expectation but the median of the band would be entered in a spreadsheet or calculation
    o   To 'enter' the expected 3-6% revenue increase in a spreadsheet one would use the median 4.5% of the reference year's known revenue levels.

Assigning values in lieu of detailed costs on a per-action or per worker basis is particularly useful in service businesses where measurements of physical inputs and outputs are not available except as broad estimates. Examples of where assigned values are logical to include (and surely illogical to knowingly not include) are:

- Where decisions can be *made faster* due to more/better/accessible info or data
- Where decisions end up being made *at lower broader levels* of the organization where service actions actually happen instead of escalating them up a hierarchy
- Where decisions are made with more inputs, causing or implying *better decisions,* less errors or less downstream review
- Where decisions and info can be shared among the *broadest employee base* and/or in the *quickest time* interval
- Where *empowered and knowledgeable employees* can make day to day decisions without delays and approvals of senior management, freeing senior management to stick to strategic and directional leadership for which they were trained and are usually highly compensated
- Where customers perform a *self serve function,* leaving employees to perform other previously unfilled work of significantly greater added value.
- Where customers *build stronger bonds* or trust in the company which in turn minimizes customer turnover and strengthens loyalty to the organization or its services, enhancing market image and goodwill

These assigned values are not goals or objectives or guesses. They are values assigned by the most logical and respected person in the organization who can be expected to intelligently state what he or she believes will be the dollar equivalent outcome of the project under study. That person's assessment should be solid, bulletproof, in that no one else inside the firm would have a better input. If more than one person has such powerful credentials and respect then a joint submission of a number or value to be assigned would occur.

Knowing your audience is useful here because assigned values are the most easily and potentially the most often challenged. You need to anticipate who will be concerned with which assigned numbers and a) try to get their understanding and alignment ahead of your meeting or publishing and b) make sure the author, the owner, of the assigned value is credible in that person's eyes.

Another source of acceptable cost information, or benefits for that matter, can be the public domain based on studies by reputable IT and Business consultancies such as Gartner Group, BCG Boston Consulting Group, A T Kearney, Deloitte, Accenture, KPMG, Cap Gemini, IDC, McKinsey from the USA; Tata Consultancy from India and PA Consulting from the UK plus several more around the world. Their observations are not published on whim, they are based on hard research and their conclusions are backed by their own reputations. Probably no big shot in your organization will disparage the findings of eminent researchers. However, YOU must be very sure that the published study relates directly to your business case and that the published conclusion is used in parallel only *in support of your case*, not instead of your case. Your organization is unique and trying to apply a cure from a peer's problem may not always be appealing or even applicable.

Where and when these values occur depends on your own organization and the type of investment you are making. In each of the above examples it will be difficult to measure the benefits and/or savings based on work units, time units or product units. Therefore it becomes important to assign, to impute, anticipated values where needed and when there is a logical corporate confidence in the approach. Examples of assigned values would be driven by logical outcomes of the above improvements would be:

- a 2-3% labour productivity increase across the division in year 1 and 2
- a 3-5% call centre sales increase by volume per year
- a 5-8% lower turnover rate of field staff per year in years 2 to 5

Be sure not to overstate any assigned values. The real accomplishment for you will to be getting your assigned subject accepted in the first place as well getting this assignment seen as conservative and reasonable. Obtaining even greater success in the project itself when completed is just that: a great success. Save something for celebrating success at the project closing party.

Each of these assigned and imputed values has a dollar equivalent that is plugged into the spreadsheets of benefits and savings, even if the median percentage number of the range is itself not the variable. Do not get too focused on small matters, too petty by including dollars that are not key to the success or failure of the project. Follow the 80:20 concept by using the 20% of costs/benefits that reflect 80% of the success and challenges in the project case.

**TIP: Remember the 80-20 rule: The assumption is that most of the results in any situation are determined by a small number of causes. Business-management consultant Joseph Juran suggested the principle and named it after Italian economist and mathematician Vilfredo Pareto, who observed in 1906 that 80% of the land in Italy was owned by 20% of the population.**

Each of these assigned or imputed values must pass a reasonableness test somewhat like those used by courts and lawyers. Such tests are described as one whereby a reasonable business person in that field would logically expect the outcome to be in the range suggested, given that person's experience, objectivity and knowledge gained in practice and through understanding the story presented in the business case. Somewhat like a jury which must decide within a 'reasonable doubt'.

Therefore such assigned values must never be 'unreasonable':

- too high to be suspect or unexpected,
- too low to be of any use or interest,
- too vague or speculative to be understood
- or based on too many variables, co-requisites or prerequisites that must also occur.

Reasonable people in your audiences must find your assertions and values reasonable, defensible; wrapped in your sincerity and supported by the subject matter expert in your organization within your business sector. All the more reason to speak with each reviewer and approver ahead of time to ensure they are reasonable and that they understand the context and intent of your use of certain data and values.

**Take Note:**   For your project make a quick list of known and understood hard and soft costs that are occurring today as part of the problem of the 'current' situation. These values will form a key part of your story that will be used to justify your business case when you write it. After all, if you can't easily determine what is wrong today, you may have major difficulty obtaining support for a project to fix the situation.

## Project Scope and the 80/20 'rule'

Your project can't do everything! The 80/20 guidance is very often used by project managers and project financial analysts. It is based on Pareto's Law and could be expressed in a number of high/low combinations such as 75/25 and 90/10 or even 87/13. The essence of the 'rule' can be expected because a small number of actions or inputs will generate a much larger result of consequences or outputs. By concentrating on the best bang objectives for the most users you would expend perhaps only 20% of the 'whole cost" and yet obtain about 80% of the beneficial outcomes. Therefore when you solicit the whole exhaustive list of wishes, you set aside the last and less important specialty applications to save 80% of the do-everything cost. Such tactics embody the 80/20 Pareto model and determine which apps get priority. If you concentrate on the key apps/outcomes then your value outcome remains optimal and you don't suffer endless pain trying to do all things for all users for all situations (possibly a never ending demand curve).

Some observers might suggest that there are a short number of variations of how the 80/20 split is interpreted for I&T, especially when a great many employees or business units lobby for their own favorite outcome. So try to balance these variations, for example:

- To deliver the 20% most effective listed outcomes and defer the 80% 'wish-list'
- To fix 75% of the problems by delivering 25% of the cures
- To eliminate 80% of errors caused by 20% of the processes (people) involved
- To suggest dismissing the 15% of employees who cause 85% of the work errors

For example, Microsoft noted that by fixing the top 20% of the most reported bugs, 80% of the errors and crashes would be eliminated (per Wikipedia April 4,2012)

And on a personal or project manager level, remember that:

- It really doesn't matter what numbers you apply, the important thing to understand is that in your life there are certain activities you do (your 20 percent) that account for the majority (your 80 percent) of your happiness and outputs.
  - (per Yaro Sarak, writer, 2006, from the *entrepreneurs-journey.com*)

Do not stray from your core scope to be friends to everyone. Extra requests beyond the solid 20% will probably crush your initial project manageability. If and when their time comes however, their needs will prove workable in a second phase project with its own ROI and NPV. As the old adage says, one must walk before one runs.

**GeoIDEA:** *If considering an introduction of a GIS/GPS based dispatch and routing application for a fleet of municipal service vehicles there are a number of current hard costs, soft costs and assigned values that might be used in your case. Hard costs today would relate to the vehicles themselves in numbers of vehicles, annual maintenance, wear and tear, depreciation and fuel usage. Softer cost would relate to driver training, salaries, overtime, vehicle age and perhaps insurance, parking fines and breakdown caused time losses. Both the hard and soft costs could likely be found with help from the accounting or finance department. Or talk with drivers and mechanics.*

*Assigned values however would be required to forecast the fuel cost increases expected, the salary rises, the legal settlements from accidents and the increased miles triggered by increased subdivisions or service demands. These latter costs may need to be assigned as no current or past history would better reflect these anticipated increased costs to the current no-routing situation.*

## ROI, NPV and PB are Financial Tools

Each investment set of cost-dollars or benefit-dollars can be combined to work out a Return on Investment, the well-known ROI if you like. We treat ROI in this broad sense of getting something back over time in exchange for the project funding. ROI is not used here in the very narrow and passive Wall Street investment banking sense of a direct profit from a bond or stock purchase and sale.

**TIP: The numbers, including financial and performance metrics, are part of the business case and are there *to support the written story*, not the other way around**

Once you set up your GIS Business Case spreadsheet workbook, it will enable you to walk through the necessary calculations for Return on Investment (ROI) and Net Present Value (NPV) on a line-by-line basis in an assumed project investment span. Payback Period (PB) is simply the number of years before the investment is paid back. PB is a restatement of the same numbers in the math of the ROI expressed in time units instead of percentage units. So while some find it useful (limited extra thinking required) it does not really add much insight to the dollar return aspect of the investment. A useful aspect of PB is that it indicates to an audience how long the disruption may last until the new project is fully embedded into the organization. As you change costs, benefits or values so too will the resultant ROI, NPV and PB change.

Gain, lose or draw! You will have your answer as to whether the proposed investment is financially desirable when the total story ends as:

- fundamentally a **money positive** one that is financially rewarding as well as enhancing the capacity and capability of the corporation OR
- essentially **money neutral** while it enhances corporate capacity or agility OR
- effectively **money negative** but still strongly justified on its alignment with corporate or strategic goals, on its building of a lasting capacity or capability and is approved based on its inherent investment and growth attributes OR
- effectively **money irrelevant** due to regulatory, legal or competitive 'must-do' reasons.

Each of these outcomes can be very effectively explained and defended whenever necessary.

While we can understand why some organizations depend greatly (solely) on financial return measures there is not and should not be a preconceived, predetermined threshold for ROI percentage or NPV amount for decision committees to approve or deny or defer projects offered by your Business Cases. The underlying math and general inability to capture truly accurate input data is too weak for such arbitrary thresholds or barriers.

Sometimes the challenge is to coordinate a keep-it-simple approach using a desired ROI number along with the reality that the core numbers themselves and therefore the resulting ROI/NPV numbers are at best 'fragile', likely 'suspect' and at worst 'wrong'. In the final analysis the numbers are rarely if ever rigorous enough to be taken as the *only measure* of foreseeable success.

One should not impose posted market based 'passive' investment returns on outcomes derived from 'active' I&T based returns, values, and impacts where added capacity and capability from GIS and I&T projects evolve over time. It is just not the same, it is comparing apples to oranges as the saying goes.

The comparison is valid only as context, as a paradigm of one concept compared to another. If the project owner or CFO actually had spare funds or no costly irritating problems would he invest in apples on the open market or would he invest in oranges to cure certain I&T health issues. Your compelling story would be key.

Another way to look at understanding how passive stock market ROI percentages should not be applied to active I&T investments is to understand that if an organizations has I&T problems causing process failures, higher costs or lower revenues then investing instead in a stock market is just plain foolish. This is not about a debate of where to invest left over cash, it is about understanding what returns in what form are to be expected from fixing a problem. They are simply not the same. They are like apples and oranges, similar but very different.

**_GeoIDEA:_** _Historically it is generally accepted in the broad GIS community that often the first few and mostly major GIS applications do not always have a positive ROI or NPV. Indeed the earlier the project, the more infrastructure, the more data conversion required and the more change management needed, making it more likely that costs will exceed short or medium term benefits and returns. However, it is equally understood that the second, third and on-going overlaid applications deliver very strong returns, many benefits at marginal costs and therefore average out the lifetime ROI at reasonable accepted levels. For an airline it costs many thousands of dollars to fly the first flight of passengers (users). A couple of years later a profit is made when the_ *flights occur 24/7/365, are full and all the training, added plug-ins and fixing of initial 'bugs' is complete. These economics apply equally to really small and very large airplanes. The same applies for really small and very large IT and GIS applications.*

Dollar denominated value is only one expression of contributed value, and usually a minority share.

The ROI and NPV numbers should give these committees and boards something to discuss, to review, to compare among projects and to face off against other goals such as strategic alignment, timing, goodwill, public image, partnership potentiality, service improvements, shareholder value and of course Green compliance and other forms of market leadership. The Business Case with all its narrative and all its figures should level the field of project explanation and justification so that the merits of each case become and remain the sole topic of discussion and evaluation as opposed to any colorful animations and charts.

## TIP: ROI and NPV would typically only weigh 20-40% on your project priority setting model

The ROI should really not be the single simple answer to any technology investment decision. It is merely the dollar denominated view of the outcome of the project's possible investment. Dollar outcome size or ratio is not always the real merit of the case. In recent years most organizations have moved away from approving GIS/IT projects based only or mostly on financial ratios such as ROI and NPV. With multi-category scoring systems that credit other compelling reasons for investing, the ROI/NPV often represents (score) only 20-40% of the weight of the project decision profile. In our RVI Portfolio model we use 35% for Returns, 35% for Values and 30% for Impacts.

**Take Note:**   If you have not done so already, take a moment to search for the definitions of four of our key words that we have used so far: Capacity and Capability; Effective and Efficient. Each of these pairs of words look and sound similar and in many ways they are. One could say they overlap somewhat. However each word has a special meaning for the Business Case writer.

The first two offer an opportunity to educate your audience on the difference between installing things (infrastructure) and sharing valuable agile intellectual property; the difference between investing in things and investing in people (knowledge). GIS/IT requires both investments. Added Capability can often utilize more Capacity of things but more things by themselves do not always create/allow more Capability.

The second two present the opportunity to educate your audience on the merits of Effectiveness in doing something better versus Efficiency in doing something faster. Both are always desirable. Both can lead to cost savings or generate higher revenues. Effective can often be Efficient but Efficient by itself is not always more Effective.

To summarize:

A positive ROI and NPV is an indicator that if all the strategic and tactical merits of the project enjoy broad support then yes, at the end of the study or project period, some sense of monetary payback will also occur. Usually the number is positive, sometimes it is not.

A negative ROI or NPV is an indicator that even if all the strategic and tactical merits of the project enjoy broad and final support, then the financial aspects must be considered an investment, an actual cost of doing business or of staying in business. Some shooters and/or financial book keeping people will use the term 'write-off' but that would be incorrect. There will be benefits, returns, values and probably operational improvements, just not enough to fully recover all the costs. Funding must come from money borrowed externally or secured from the internal annual budget process (e.g. from shared contributions of each participating department or division).

In itself a low or possibly negative ROI or NPV does not automatically negate a project's value. Like in any other business decision ... "it depends" on the context in which the company finds itself... at this time.

## **Invest to improve data and access to it**

Base benefits of I&T (including GIS) investments normally fall into only three categories:

- Facilitating increased *revenue generation*
  - the top three concepts here are to:
    - sell more current products to <u>existing customers</u> within current areas of business using pricing, marketing and sales efforts
    - sell current products to <u>new customers</u> in current and new areas of business located by the GIS
    - sell <u>new products</u> to existing and newly found customers in current and new areas of business

- Enabling *process improvements* which improve the design and delivery of services and which could also encourage customer loyalty or employee retention
  - the top three approaches here are:
    - The transfer of employee labour to self-serve customers from employees (e.g. encourage internet users to use your eCommerce)
    - The use of GIS/IT resources to replace human resources when more efficient (e.g. routing software to save drive times and gasoline)
    - The increased effectiveness of employee paid hours (e.g. increase levels of authority for GIS analysts to publish operational guidance based on the research which in turn may make business unit decisions more effective, less wrong, less often appealed to senior management and so on)

- Creating *savings* in operations or other expense categories:
  - The top three ideas here are to:
    - Do existing work at less cost (e.g. less employees, maybe more overtime)
    - Do more work at existing cost levels (e.g. use bonuses and other employee incentives; higher up-time for internet servers)
    - Hire GIS/IT Business Case consultants instead of using dated habits and poor methods that do not recognize the effectiveness and efficiencies of building capacity and capability across the enterprise.

A better informed workforce is more effective and therefore more efficient. A better informed workforce is typically happier and more satisfied at work. Satisfied workers perform better. A better informed decision is a more efficient or effective decision. A better informed decision is made sooner, with less deliberation, less time consuming internal consultation (debate) with co-workers and others. Therefore the workforce at all levels of the organization becomes more efficient and delivers better service. A well informed customer base can be seen as more loyal to the firm or to the firm's products and services. Desired outcomes of investments can include corporate peer level competitive advantage or catch-up.

Additionally, new worker knowledge with its concurrent effectiveness and satisfaction can minimize staff turnover thus avoiding significant downstream costs. Enhancing the workday of employees and/or the customer experience becomes a mission accomplished. Top quality data delivered effectively is the 'best practice' catalyst for this to happen.

It has often been observed in enterprise I&T projects and programs that "if you build it they will come". This idea often proves true, not just because of the underlying ROI or NPV values but because major enterprise projects gather support and momentum as they develop, as they mature. When this support creates new savings or new uses of the prior application, the value and returns improve. Some commentators might suggest that over time the secondary (softer) benefits can surpass those of the primary ones identified in the business case. Approvers need to understand the lag effect of such continuing secondary benefits even while they focus overly on the more immediate primary ones.

A May 2009 paper distributed freely by IBM/Cognos entitled *"Improving confidence by increasing understanding in information"* identifies that the path followed for information is from <u>Understanding</u> to <u>Trust</u> to <u>Relevance</u>. We could expand on that to suggest that in Geographic Information Systems recently enhanced data goes from:

- awareness to
  - familiarity to
    - accessibility to
      - understanding to
        - trust and confidence to
          - effective usage

And of course *effective usage* means sharing broadly and basing actions and decisions upon the best information. When the decision inputs such as demographic data by area are broadly shared and understood, the general acceptance of the decision itself increases, buy-in increases, response improves. It's human nature, it's good management and it's a best practice ... in action.

Build it and they will come is evidenced when users that were sometimes overlooked or misinformed during the initial needs assessment speak up in mid project or even later to demand inclusion and access. Remember that there must be a compelling business story and financial contribution before you build it in the first place. The benefit seems to be an outcome that post-development adoption and employee utility is much higher than pre-project needs assessments typically identify. Again, applications such as GIS, ERP and BI can be cited.

***Take Note***:    Contact some front line customer facing employees to find out what types of location based information they know would be useful and valuable but also know it is not currently available to them. Alternatively imagine yourself calling a contact center or standing at a service counter and imagine how much better equipped (capable) an employee could be in serving you if they only had full location based profile data about you or your account. Sometimes a boost to a business case comes when writers assume the role of consumers, enquire from the outside and learn quickly how poorly their organization is unable to serve them better.

# ABOUT THE FINANCIAL MEASURES

Asking what the preferred financial measures are for you organization is a very important question. The answer should be put in the context of how useful, how valid, how important financial measures are in judging and scoring all I&T and GIS projects. More importantly, any financial measure stated as an objective or expectation assumes to a large degree that the project team will be able to isolate the benefits afterwards and that other changes will have not occurred in the organization during the project period. Naturally there is almost no sure way to look back and prove what the ROI or NPV actually was. This is why post project reassessments are rarely done. Of course so much else will change during the project timeline that there will be little or no way to break out the positive financial impact strictly derived from the project alone.

That is not to suggest that post-project reviews and audits should be forsaken. Rather it suggests we should advise up front how we will check later:

- on the project costs themselves versus expectations (money and people)
- on the values of capacity and capability that have been created (before and after)
- on the impacts on employees (how and how many) and customers (how and how often)
- on the regulatory preparedness or compliance that is now possible
- on Business Intelligence reports to corporate leaders (new actionable content)

The intent to do so and the anticipated methods for doing so can be included in your business case document under Section 9 General Plan for Project Resources and should be mentioned in Section 2, in your Executive Summary.

So ranking GIS and IT proposals, using a framework for all IT projects, usually gives a 15-35 percent weight to financial parameters (weights above 30% are attributed only when the project motivation is overwhelmingly financial) and gives the remaining weight to non-monetary growth (like values and impacts reflecting improved capability, agility, capacity and robustness). It will be important for you to communicate that the best financial measures are never fully reliable. So don't base your project's life solely on ROI and NPV financial measures. You must find additional benefits to substantiate the business case.

All three of the ROI, NPV and PB measures use essentially the same input numbers which reflect:

- all expected project costs (initial and during the project study lifecycle)
- all expected benefits (input and process savings, revenues) for the study life and
- all anticipated values assigned on a department, division or corporate level

The time allocated to the project lifecycle is typically 1 to 3 to 5 years. Looking beyond five years is so very difficult in this rapidly changing world. Lifting the project horizon to longer outlooks should only be taken if absolutely necessary and then preferably with simple extrapolation of percentages. By using and admitting to simple arithmetic extrapolation, the business case author is alerting readers to the frailty of the underlying research, data, conclusions and expectations. Like most strategies, the direction of growth or success might be well described, but the level and timing of actual successes are not solid. This is again because detailed future statements imply an accuracy level and underlying supported analysis that is rarely possible in real business life.

We recommend that all salary numbers be stated as "fully loaded" or "encumbered" to include standard budgetary overheads, such as vacation, illness, pension contribution and other, which can typically account for an additional 25-30% of each salary hour and can be higher than 40% in some cases. The company may pay someone $30,000 of salary per year but they might actually cost $39,000 due to a 30% overhead loading factor. All project purchases would generally not include sales taxes as they are often not a financial consideration, but this would differ in varying countries. Some may be as high as 50% and you must decide whether to use the standard or soften it in the isolated circumstances of your project case. Contractor dollars may not be loaded at all as they often come 'all-in'. Your accounting manager can advise you.

ROI represents the yield from the total project investment and is calculated from the total cash flows generated by the benefits, less the total project cost cash flows divided by the total cost cash flows, minus ONE, yielding a percentage. The ONE is deducted as it represents the first year that is included. Our view is that the percentage should ideally be a band (e.g. 8-10%) or if necessary a whole number (e.g. 9%).

**TIP: The resultant ROI should not be quoted with decimals because any decimal will imply a precision and an investigative rigor that simply does not exist. Decision makers need to know when a number is precise, such as an interest rate on a GIC, and they need to be clear when the number is actually the "best available", less precise or even much less precise, such as an ROI return on an I&T investment.**

ROI has a twin brother called IRR or Internal Rate of Return. Some organizations prefer IRR because it is quoted as a percentage, it reflects internal versus external outcomes and it puts NPV in percentage terms. IRR is the percentage return that brings the NPV to zero. As such it bridges the ROI percentage concept to the NPV money pile concept. For our purposes in this book, however, we will stick with ROI and NPV as preferred choices.

NPV represents the bottom line value of the project to the firm, the net benefit less costs, brought back to the assumed present day. It is like pretending that the entire project took place today so you can set aside all issues caused by the passage of time. NPV is calculated by subtracting all the costs from all the benefits over each project period and by discounting the cost of money disbursements over the project lifecycle. NPV determines what the assumed positive net benefit will be when expressed as a sum of money (e.g. $2.2M) in today's time. See above regarding NPVs sister, the IRR.

## TIP: Of the two, the preferred measure in the minds of many I&T and GIS observers is NPV, Net Present Value.

ROI is the most famous measure and ironically it is also often the least appropriate.  Other publications such as magazines and journals often discuss the debate on why this happens. Suffice to suggest here that ROI is better for Wall Street for stock analysts to compare simpler passive investments over a fairly short defined time period of a known fixed investment. I&T projects are not like that, they are complex and active, they get adopted over time in phases and they start wearing down right away, even if they take five years to be replaced.

The historical irony of ROIs aura in technology investments is that humans have too often tended to overstate revenue estimates and savings while understating costs and timelines. Thus the expected ROI was never possible and likely never traceable or proven.

On a more practical level, ROI can be tough for some people to imagine, to envisage as a result. Not everyone can 'see' the difference between a return of 7% and of 11% for a $1.7836 million dollar project. It is even harder for some to envisage a negative number such as minus six percent (-6%). This can be even more difficult to perceive if the major reason for the negative is also intangible, like taxes, depreciation and interest as opposed to labor or equipment. The bottom line of a business case is better and faster approval if it is better understood.

Of the two, the preferred financial measure in the minds of many I&T and GIS observers is NPV, Net Present Value. NPV tells us what the net cash in hand will be, today, in the present, of all types of benefits over the project period minus all types of costs over the project period. NPV can be 'seen', imagined, as a tangible material result: an amount of cash "earned"; a pile of dollar bills; a box of Euros if you like. ROI is only a percentage, a concept, an abstract number with less sense of whether that number is good, better or not. NPV works really well if the NPV is positive with cash left over in a figurative cashbox or the CEO's hand. Similarly the bundle of cash cost "invested" is imagined as it leaves the firm, the hand, when the NPV is negative.

Even if your organization is a public service less interested in "profit" or present value, this NPV measure enables senior managers to sense the size, to see the money pile, of the investment they are making. Everyone reports to someone and the need to describe the beneficial outcome of any I&T or GIS investment project is still very real in the private sector or public sector or anywhere in between.

PB, or PayBack period is different in that it simply tells you how fast you earned enough benefits to cover your costs. Be aware though that PayBack period does not speak directly to whether this length of time is good, good enough or not good. It is what it is, that's all. If the ROI or NPV is negative, no net cash pay back, the PB period cannot be determined.

Many I&T projects do not ever earn direct net profits. Often they just keep things "on". Many simply cannot be precisely analyzed post-completion in order to determine what returns actually occurred. Some therefore 'lose' money and become more like costs of doing business than true financial investments. Negative ROI numbers seem to scare people before they take the time to understand the broader implications of investing in keeping the business functioning, i.e. maintaining capacity. Negative NPV numbers are easily understood and accepted as expenditures for 'keeping the lights on' or maybe 'to keep the roof from leaking'. While brackets and minus signs can sometimes trigger negative thoughts or negative criticism it must be remembered that in work life as well as in home life, some improvements simply cost money to remain current, to avoid getting all wet.

## Definitions and more!

This book is not meant to teach finance, accounting arithmetic nor advanced math. We are simply sharing the context and the characteristics of successful I&T business cases. We understand that every organization has financial managers and other experts that know how to calculate important ratios such as ROI, NPV and PB. We also understand that these people must be integrated into the project by the business case authors to ensure all industry and regulatory rules are followed. They will dictate what interest rates and depreciation schedules to use, what tax rates will apply and which expenses will be considered 'capital costs' and which will be considered 'expense costs'.

The role of the business case writer therefore includes getting help from financial experts once the research and findings about costs, savings and assigned values are known. At that point, only the financial math remains to be completed and those financial experts can assist and by extension become spokespersons for the correctness of the final measures. Remember, the numbers support the story. So the financial managers support the case writers who are the story tellers. If your financial measures and calculations are from the Finance Department, they are more bullet-proof.

As noted, this book is not trying to train readers to be finance or engineering operatives, even though many of you may already be proficient in those fields. Those wishing to fully understand the detailed financial calculations, using interest rates over time periods and reflecting inflation and other financial fine points should obtain direct advice in their work location or on websites such as Wikipedia.org (which requests donations from users).

### ROI: Return on Investment

According to Wikipedia May 15, 2013

*"return on investment = (gain from investment - cost of investment) / cost of investment"*

**and also**

*"Return on Investment (ROI) is one of the most popular performance measurement and evaluation metrics used in business analysis. ROI analysis (when applied correctly) is a powerful tool for evaluating existing information systems and making informed decisions on software acquisitions and other projects. However, ROI is a metric designed for a certain purpose – to evaluate profitability or financial efficiency. It cannot reliably substitute for many other financial metrics in providing an overall economic picture of the information solution. The attempts at using ROI as the sole or principal metric for decision making regarding information systems cannot be productive. It may be appropriate in a very limited number of cases/projects. ROI is a financial measure and does not provide information about efficiency or effectiveness of the information systems."*

These are thoughts we find useful. ROI is a good metric of the simple result of dividing the net gain of the investment by the cost of the investment and expecting a return, hopefully in the 5-20% range. But because so many values and dollars in the equation are not fully proven, the result can be tainted even if heartily adopted by some managers. The second point is interesting in that it cautions us that the efficacy of the investment is not for ROI to measure. This encourages us to look deeper in our RVI model which will do in a book later in 2013.

## *NPV: Net Present Value*

According to Wikipedia May 15, 2013

*"NPV can be described as the "difference amount" between the sums of discounted: cash inflows and cash outflows. It compares the present value of money today to the present value of money in future, taking inflation and returns into account"*

NPV can be imagined or described in a story as being a pile of cash earned by improving processes and using less money to deliver new processes than the savings from the stoppage of the old processes.

Note: a ratio called IRR or Internal Rate of Return is that interest rate (e.g. 9%) which is derived to make the NPV zero. In other words, when your investment of $200,000 ends up with an NPV of $18,000 (simply stated) the IRR is 9% because that percentage times the costs would make the NPV zero. Ironically, this removes the advantage of NPV as an understandable end result, a pile of cash earned.

Per Wikipedia (Feb 2013): *"IRR calculations are commonly used to evaluate the desirability of investments or projects. The higher a project's IRR, the more desirable it is to undertake the project. Assuming all projects require the same amount of up-front investment, the project with the highest IRR would be considered the best and undertaken first."*

### PB: PayBack Period

PB = PayBack period which is the time duration (years or months) that it takes for the value of the total benefits to replace the project costs. Identify when total savings and benefits to date have accumulated to be equal to costs to date plus total remaining costs (if more coming) and divide by the number of months since the project started. Reasonable outcomes are between 18 to 36 months for small projects and 24 to 48 months for larger ones. We recall the US Government accepting a 35 year payback for the building (and many years of developmental maintenance) of the US National Map because it would take that long to build and ensure effective sharing and utilization throughout the economy. Governments can accept such longer payback periods because their role is to encourage progress and to create assets that build capacity and capability. There is no ideal. The dichotomy is obvious: payback is simply a good thing while not paying back is not necessarily a bad thing.

However if your project business case, even if expertly written and bullet-proof as it can be, does not generate a positive financial ratio then clearly the investment must demonstrably create capacity and capability for near or future strategic, legal or regulatory reasons, despite the costs.

A series of spreadsheets as described in Section 7 will help you to take care of the math.

**Remember**: it is the narrative that explains and justifies the project investment; the math and ratios are there to add the monetary clarity, including scope and size, to the business story.

Straightforward ROI, NPV and PB calculations are done as above and are sufficient for most preliminary financial estimates for an I&T project. However, many organizations expect much more mathematical rigor which includes interest rates, time, depreciation, inflation, taxes and other overheads. In these cases it is strategically wise to engage your finance or accounting department advisors so that the generally accepted factors are included and so that those advisors can attest that you have indeed performed a rigorous analysis. Again, the numbers support the narrative strategic value story of why a project is recommended and submitted for approval.

The compelling business rationale is the story and the financial benefit levels are supportive explanations which are required for prioritizing or ranking which project to fund first, second etc.

***Take Note*:**   Contact someone in your accounting or finance groups and find out if there is any corporate bias or prerequisite for or against the use of ROI, IRR, NPV or PB so that you can prepare correctly. Be prepared to use the favorite measures as well as NPV. When you write your case be certain not to overpromise financial gains that cannot be measured or worse, cannot realistically be met.

**TIP: Precise future numbers, dollars and volumes are never available. You must present acceptable 'best available' numbers in making your case. You must know their pedigree. You then own them, they become yours and you must shield them from random or targeted bullets and doubters.**

## Managing Expectations from Estimates, Forecasts and Projections

Being bullet-proof requires at the very least not setting oneself up as a target. The best targets are usually numbers because audiences are free to judge not only the number itself but the author of the number and the original owner of the number. Either personal bias or a lack of appreciation for the orders of magnitude of some numbers can lead a reviewer to disagree with even the best researched number, just because they wish to.

A major error often made by business case writers is to allow, or create, insurmountable fears when stating numbers, especially regarding the project costs, potential lost revenues, disaffected customers, potential lawsuits and employee resignations. Big numbers can be very scary unless introduced carefully or avoided when describing what 'might' happen. David Eddie, a journalist in Canada's Globe and Mail newspaper, described in late 2012 his disregard for out of sense statistics by referring to them as "speculatistics" or "speculative statistics". Such numbers used in advertising or in selling your project Eddie would call "advertistics" and hold in equal dislike. Be sure your stated numbers do not appear speculative or hyped for advertizing. Make sure you know their pedigree, history, context and usability to avoid being shot down over a number that got too much reaction.

At the early stages of a business case for I&T one has to determine what the expected costs and the expected savings/benefits will be over the project's study period. Actual numbers do not become available in advance of a project. Therefore your financial and operations arithmetic will require manual adjustments, or what we earlier called "assigned values". It is imperative therefore that you identify the source of any such adjusted inputs, or assigned values, and the rationale behind using them.

A technique that can be helpful is to be diligent, picky perhaps, in differentiating among such everyday terms as 'estimate', 'forecast' and 'projection'. We try not to use the word 'guess' because there is no need to do so, even in extreme situations. In our personal lives we tend to use these three terms loosely and interchangeably. In a business case we should use them carefully and each in its own context because these are usefully different from each other and should ideally be recognized as such. No matter which one you use for any purpose, be sure to state what kind of number it is and to attribute the source of your number, whether from a staff member, a third party, an outside reference or a retained subject matter expert, SME or consultant.

We suggest the following uses for these 3 expectations:

An **ESTIMATE** is defined as *an approximate judgment* in the Oxford Dictionary. It would be a number deemed reasonable by you as the case writer or a by a known SME who may be an internal employee subject matter expert or an external commentator. The estimate itself would be in the order of magnitude of acceptable ranges for such numbers and reflect the nature of the subject of the project. It may be stated as a range such as 1-3% or 3-7%, with wider ranges indicating higher degrees of concern about the accuracy of the number.

- Example: the call centre manager *estimates* a 2-4 lower complaint call volume per year if this project proceeds as described. It is her considered opinion, being the operational subject expert for this matter. It should be quite bullet-proof because the best expert in the company made the estimate.
  - Be absolutely certain to state who made this estimate, with what on-the-job credibility and with which caveats if any
  - Better still to be able to quote supporting evidence from media reports, verified vendor assertions or peer papers or

vendor press releases of similar success in other organizations

A **FORECAST** is a view forward; *a conjectural prediction of something future* says the Oxford Dictionary. It is affected by assumed factors of growth or shrinkage. Forecasts are by nature ... always wrong. The hope is to be not far wrong and not in the less desirable direction.

- Example: Sales to customers are forecast by the product management team to grow by 30,000 units per year, representing approximately a 4 percent growth.
  - Keep it logically reasonable, imaginable, believable and therefore defensible while you name the forecaster(s).
  - Even better when the forecast is team based and not reliant on just one individual, no matter how knowledgeable that one person is.

A **PROJECTION** is *a derived figure* per the Oxford Dictionary and is usually (at least) based on past figures, projected forward under identified terms and conditions.

- Example: call volumes have been growing at 2% per year for six years and are expected to continue on that scale, growing by 165,000 over 3 years if this project does not proceed at this time.
  - Identify the basis of the projection, the time-line and the multiplier because your reader will test you, it's human nature again
  - Better still to put this type of number in an imaginable picture such as: 165 thousand added calls equates to over seven added and trained contact centre employees plus one supervisor requiring over 1100 square feet of additional equipped office space and five parking spots.

Using these approaches is appropriate when inputting numbers to your spreadsheet. In your narrative you must always identify the source (e.g. a certain manager, a trade journal study, an academic survey or a quote from a related context) and therefore the strength of the numbers, whether estimated, forecast or projected. This is critical. Never just guess and always avoid being accused of guessing by being confident that you have the best available numbers. If they are the best available numbers, you are shielded and bullets can't hit you.

**Take Note:** Think of some performance indicator in your department and how it might be seen to change over the next 3 years if you had to predict the new result. Do so in terms of each estimate, forecast and projection. Try to understand the differences as well as the similarities and how defending each is slightly different.

**GeoIDEA:** *Showing ROI and NPV in GIS projects that are core or are early in the lifecycle of using GIS has eluded most managers. Initial costs have too often proven to be quite high due to the need for data cleanup and storage as well as broad communication bands. Examples may include utility planning projects in the 1990s, government shared GIS programs, early vehicle routing w/o GPS).*

*Regrettably those outcomes have made GIS memorable for the wrong reasons. However, secondary and smaller projects in later phases that were built on those initial investments actually produced excellent value and payback and have been positively memorable for their subsequent success. So be prepared to discuss this GIS image when some people take shots at GIS in general and your expected project in particular. Better to be prepared to name other firms whose early projects were quite successful and where continued benefits can be seen today (examples may include GPS based logistics/routing; utility asset management; retail marketing; natural resource management; municipal planning and others).*

# Time Value of Money: Interest Rates, Time and Inflation

Professional finance managers and accountants in your organization may at some point want to factor in inflation, interest rate variations or any other aspect of what is called the Time Value of Money.

Set these aside for now. Do not factor them into your early analysis. This is because in a Business Case we are taking a preliminary look at the essence of the case to explain and financially support a project. Inflation is a projected value, an expectation and so is best left out of preliminary business cases, especially when the projected rate is very low.

However be aware that some organization's financial groups may prefer to have these included before presenting your case for approval. If so be sure to track what happens to your overall economics with and without these factors, in case the difference is significant. For example if a high interest rate or inflation rate is used, or a too short project time is forced on you, the bottom line ROI and NPV could be quite lower. So when the low NPV is discussed it is important to note that one or more of these factors is critical and a discussion on their merits and size can be initiated. The effect will be there no matter what but as author of the case you need to know the 'why' behind the 'what' for your analysis results.

Interest rates are very similar to Inflation. They might somewhat affect both costs and benefits over time if fluctuations are wide, as will many other potential external factors. So just as the economist prefers to "hold other things constant" to show the isolated impact of a policy or single variable change, so too do you want to study your project with all "other things equal", or "held constant". To an I&T business case writer, it is generally accepted that a dollar is a dollar and one this year is the same as one next year or the year after. To a similar extent a dollar from business operations and a dollar borrowed is the same dollar, so while interest charges may become directly applicable, a judgment call should be made to ask if they are significant enough to factor into the business case, *at the time of writing*. Typically they are not.

**No decimals please!** They are your worst enemy. They create undue pressures when ironically you are trying to be insightful and strategic. It is like the joke about quoting your age: when you turn 12 you answer 'going on 13'; when you are almost 30 you say 'just 29' and when you are 69 you say 'in my sixties'. But people hearing you will make their own judgment. So when you use decimals, people will round up benefits, round down costs, average time periods and forget all your warnings. Don't let them control the memory of your number. Spreadsheets will generate decimals often, so truncate or round the answers and then state them in your 'up to', 'approximate' and 'expected to be about' phrases.

Because so many Business Case inputs are estimated, forecast, projected and then maybe assigned, there is little true benefit in using outputs with decimal places. The reason is that when human beings see two, three or more decimal places in a result it leads them to subconsciously believe or assume there was a rigor, a depth of mathematical research and accuracy that simply is not there. Much as the Richter Scale adds apparent accuracy to earthquakes and tremors, 6.7 versus 6.8, as a power of ten increase, so does stating your expected number as a decimal imply a power of ten accuracy. But Richter is measured by multiples of the best of scientific electronics while your business case math is not and cannot be.

Such precision simply can't be determined as early as the business case preparation time. Remember what really matters … the building of confidence, capability and capacity in your organization. Dollar denominated ratios and their images of payback help explain what is expected to happen, all else held constant, but they do not in themselves deliver value of merit to the organization. So decimal places should not be required.

Numbers that are estimates, projections of forecasts should be whole numbers and preferably should be in bands e.g. 11% or 10-12%. Executive confidence in your case derives from your own confidence and your energetic defense of the order of magnitude of your whole number (e.g. 11% versus 15% or 9%) or the narrowness of your band (e.g. 10-12% versus 9-15%). This is where the role of Contingencies and Sensitivities is critical. Because your case includes these factors, your bottom line 'return' expectations are well framed and defensible. You and your numbers will be respected as 'reasonable'.

## Contingency Funds and Sensitivity Analyses

These two concepts are similar but significantly different in impact on decision making for project approvals. They are both generally helpful when well understood but can be unhelpful if confused or improperly handled.

CONTINGENCY dollars are additional amounts of up to 10% of the whole that are usually added to the bottom of the list of costs to allow for all the little items that you forgot to include or were wrongly advised would not apply. It is an amount of cash for a "just in case" surprise or oversight. It is a reflection on your openness and integrity that the ROI/NPV math may have omitted something or misquoted some amount. Just in case, plug in 10%. You'll likely use it! But if you are tempted to use contingencies above 10% then get back to hard work and find out more details and more prices of what might be involved. A business case with too high an amount of "just in case" money is not defensible and will be shot full of bullet holes by many reviewers. Contingency dollars are real dollars included in the budget request because you do expect to need them.

SENSITIVITY factors are alternative value factors used for any heavily weighted key cost or major benefit in the event that your original value is terribly wrong. It applies most when there are one or two, maybe three, key cost accounts where each is shown to be at least 15% of the total budget weight and where wide fluctuations may be out of your control or predictability: e.g. overtime salaries or fuel consumption.

Sensitivity analysis is used to demonstrate what happens *if* the one variable in question turns out to be *dramatically* higher or lower than expected. It is a reflection on your wisdom and insight to recognize that some variables are so important that major shifts in their outcomes could significantly alter the project success. So rerun your math by substituting each of a 10%, 15% or even 30% <u>higher</u> value for one key variable at a time to see if this delta in itself has a material effect on the bottom line of your project. Then do the same for each of 10%, 15% and 30% <u>lower</u> values for this variable. React to what you learn when doing this. Deal with it if the effect on the overall project numbers are indeed major.

For example if the server array component was 40% of the total project expense predicted, and this one category were to be 15% too low (for example an unforeseen price increase) then in fact this one component could <u>on its own</u> turn the project from positive to negative. Consideration would then be given to mitigating this risk or at worst, not proceeding with the project under these circumstances. If there are in fact no major disproportionate sub-sets of factors on which to perform a sensitivity analysis then it would be appropriate to do one, at a lower "if" factor of 5% or so, on the entire cost side or benefit side amount.

Sensitivity analyses are not just to avoid bad news. In fact as often as not the uptake on new data available is higher than expected and so a study to weigh the implications of significantly added success is just as valuable. The sensitivity dollars do not become a real portion of the requested budget except where a sensitized budget is preferred to ensure higher funds are available for the 'what if'.

In summary: a Contingency is a 5-10% factor of total cost inputs to accommodate unspecified but generally expected total expenditures or benefits/revenue losses. Sensitivity is a 10-30% factor run against specific high impact sub-categories of costs and/or benefits to ensure that surprises in these singular categories do not seriously affect the whole project.

A business case author should include both of these, no matter how approximate, to avoid surprises and to demonstrate breadth as well as depth in the supporting numbers used in the case document. There is always one reviewer who loves to ask about these 'what if scenarios' and she must be answered **before** she asks the question.

- *Contingency* is NOT the same as *Sensitivity*.
  - The contingency added to the sub-total is for <u>just in case</u>
  - The plus/minus sensitivity of key inputs is for <u>what if.</u>

**Take Note:** Identify a project that you believe had or should have had both a contingency factor and one or more sensitivity factors. Write down how you would describe the factors and how you might explain each to a committee of review.

*GeoIDEA: GIS project memories are full of sensitivity costs because for so long there was little history. Change management may seem easy when you think of how GPS friendly our populations are today versus twenty years ago. However there can be a big difference in learning curves for using a simple GPS unit in your car versus fully understanding how to overlay location coordinates on a sales-by-volume mapping application in the marketing department. of data points and your costs could skyrocket. So be sure to allow for such Sensitivities and to double your efforts to get the right forecast up front. Similarly, sensitivities could be applied to hard to measure human work efficiency such as in-field data capture. Software and hardware expenses should be very accurately predictable as long as they are sized appropriately.*

*On the Contingency curve one should watch out for the need to add in a simple 5-10-15% for the whole project simply because humans tend to underestimate costs always. Test scores and revenue opportunities seem to be overly anticipated by these same humans. It's a feature of our central processors.Less so today but when you have a large number of data items (points by the millions, lines by the many thousands and polygons by the thousands) the labour and other costs can multiply very quickly. It would be easy to be 20% wrong in either direction, 30% even. Multiply an extra minute of human or machine updating times millions.*

## Sunk Costs and Opportunity Costs

The mention of these two types of special 'costs' is fairly common in investment analysis because people can be confused about money spent on earlier projects or money that could be spent on alternate projects when they review your specific project's business case. Again you might get help from your internal professional money managers in Finance or Accounting. This is always helpful to those trying to understand the mysteries of accounting. These two types of costs are usually omitted from an I&T Business Case.

### Sunk Costs

Sunk Costs are, in plain English, monies that are already spent and cannot be recovered. They are gone, finished, sunk.

According to About.com (June 2009)

- "Sunk costs are unrecoverable past expenditures (which) should not normally be taken into account when determining whether to continue a project or abandon it, because they cannot be recovered either way. It is a common instinct to count them, however."

For I&T and GIS projects it can be very tempting and surely interesting to know that a new application will use the desktop computers that were bought last month according to the equipment refreshment program. But we don't need to add these costs to our new project. We are going forward. The computers are already bought and paid for. Accountants call these "sunk costs" and your business case document should identify the computer use for your project, but no costs would be allocated. Your narrative could state your pleasure that such added costs do not apply this time and no allocation is needed in your current business case. The financial benefit to the organization is that more value will be gained from the earlier expense of buying new computers. The ROI on that other and past project now glows brighter.

## Opportunity Costs

Opportunity costs are those related to choosing a different opportunity or solution. These are costs you may wish to describe in your document. These are "costs" imputed for not doing something else that might have been viable or even expected. Opportunity cost descriptions can be useful when they suggest alternative decisions or different plans that may have seemed logical or desirable but were mutually exclusive to each other and to the proposed business case choice. It is a tricky concept for sure.

Per Investopedia.com on June 24, 2009

- an opportunity cost is that cost of an alternative that is foregone in order to pursue your chosen project or action. It identifies the benefits you could have received by taking a different decision.

For example: if you invest in a new truck and it saves 2% on fuel costs because of its new efficient motor, but you gave up the opportunity to buy the hybrid which would have saved 6% on fuel then your opportunity costs are 4% (6% less 2%). And yes please assume that the two vehicles had the same price tag.

Opportunity costs are often described in the business case narrative to make the point about the other opportunity not taken, to preclude a question likely to be asked, but usually the dollar cost is not included in the financial aspects because these 'costs' are often 'theoretical' or 'virtual' numbers. A sort of triple negative: you do not count the costs you did not save by not taking the other option. Yes it can be awkward and confusing without actually enhancing your business case story. Make sure the subject is really important and useful to explore, or just leave it out by design. You can then focus on why you left it out as opposed to why it is worth leaving in. Another tough defense.

## Risk and Risk Mitigation for the Project

Most organizations of medium, large or super size have a risk model, probably a risk mitigation plan and sometimes a dedicated risk officer. This definition of risk tends to be at the corporate wide level to deal with major environmental, political, market driven risks. In this book we are focused only on risks related directly to the proposed project described in our business case narrative.

The whole subject of both corporate risk and our own project risk is often summarized as follows in two estimates, one of likelihood (probability) and one of consequence (damage).

- What is the likelihood that our project will suffer or fail because of one or more occurrences or problems that we can name?
- What is the expected damage level that such an occurrence, if it happens, will cause?

As an illustration, let us simply describe a typical I&T/GIS project case issue that could land within the low to high 'risk' continuum.

Our project will rely on the delivery of 400 new rugged notebook computers for our outside maintenance worker crews to be delivered 3 months before project cutover. The risk scenarios are that they may be late by two weeks, one month or a few months. The impact or effect on the project will be described as:

- LOW or NOT CONCERNED if there is little or no impact to the project. For example, if they are two weeks late, that is viewed as quite manageable; any number of other project items may be two weeks behind at that time anyway and this delay would not, of its own, hurt the then current schedule dramatically so carry on with all efforts. Think of a Green traffic light.
- MEDIUM or CAUTION if there is some impact to the project. For example, if they are late by one month, it will require alternate risk-mitigating actions to be taken to manage the delay; project management costs to revamp the schedule of

software loading, testing and employee training may be required. Quite manageable. Think of a Yellow traffic light.
- HIGH or SERIOUS if there is significant impact to the project. For example, if they are late by more than two months it may be necessary to postpone related activities that could actually trigger project delays, costs or even a rush to secure an alternate supplier along with legal action against the initial supplier. Such a delay may directly trigger higher purchase costs or lower/delayed service benefits as well. Action and notifications will be required. Think Red light.

Business case writers and analysts should consider very strongly how 'time' factors into the risk assessment. Where the likelihood of a risk may be strong but the advance warning time is long, the risk itself may be quite manageable. On the one hand if the risk matter is short-fused or volatile then the risk magnitude may be greater because little or no prevention or repair time may be available. In our view warning time is fundamental to project risk models, sometimes more than likelihood (probability) and consequence (damage). Many risk models fail to fully account for such warning time and response time aspect.

*Take Note*:    For your project make a quick list of known, understood risk factors that may occur today. These risks will form a key part of your story. They will be used to justify your actions to raise alarms or set a risk management plan in your business case. After all, if you can't easily determine and describe what might be a problem today, you may have major difficulty obtaining support for a project to fix the situation.

*GeoIDEA*:    *Standard project risks of course apply to GIS projects. Lessons from internationally accepted standards and educational organizations such as ITIL\* and COBIT\* and PMI\* are full of lessons learned. You should ask yourself for a GIS project what extra risks are possible because of anticipated data licensing from third parties and* *local governments; what liability issues occur from these people too. Similarly what added, or maybe lessened risk occurs if your project is partnered with co-requisite projects or those of related agencies with whom your processes are inter-related. GIS is a discipline that tends to have more outside partners and cooperators than most other applications. So be extra careful in determining and measuring project risk. That will also protect corporate risk at the same time.*

- *ITIL stands for Information Technology Infrastructure Library
- *COBIT stands for Control OBjectives for Information and Related Technology
- *PMI stands for the Project Management Institute

# IDENTIFYING FINANCIALS for YOUR SUPPORT WORKBOOK

Listed below in bullet form are a variety of standard themes, titles, types and variations of costs, benefits and assigned values that your business case could identify, describe and explain. Dollars and volume numbers for these variables should be entered by you on an appropriate worksheet template in order to calculate a ROI or NPV when appropriate.

One of the best ways to gather this information is to create a matrix table or use a spreadsheet. Start with paper if you must but end up in digital format. Simply list the cost categories down the left column, and list the departments or functions across the top. Use the maximum number of column and row titles as you can at first. Later you can consider combining titles (and adding their numbers together) because when you look at your gathered data you no doubt will see where certain titles/numbers reflect essentially the same activity. For example you may begin by tracking airplane costs and taxi fares separately because they are different activities. Before long you realize that many taxi fares occur to and from the airport and transportation is transportation. So you combine the two. Hotel fees look special at first but before long you realize that hotel stays usually accompany flights and taxis. So you combine these as 'travel'. And so on.

So you try to be as granular as possible at first. As you fill in the boxes and cells with tick marks, Yes/No indicators or money amounts you will gradually build an extremely valuable data file for your case subject as it applies across the entire organization. That is so highly valuable in itself and will enable you to avoid almost all bullets just by virtue of knowing who does what currently, how often, how well and at what price.

Fantastic!

By virtue of this research you have become the most knowledgeable employee subject matter expert, the most bullet-proof operations researcher and soon-to-be problem solver in the firm. For a while at any rate, so enjoy it will you can.

We leave it to you to put these results in their logical context in your particular workplace. Only you and your associates will know if the resulting financial measures hold meaning to you and whether each result indicated enough support for pursuing the proposed project, or when, or to what degree.

## Costs

Don't forget, you have to build a full matrix of operational and other costs by activity by volume by department which is applicable to the current situation, the one you want to change. You also will build a second full matrix of costs that will be incurred during the project as part of new purchases, conversion activities and the management of change. You will have a third matrix of new and continuing operational costs in the post project period.

In the most simplified sense, the net result of the third worksheet matrix less the first worksheet matrix is your first simplified look at the operational savings portion of your proposal. If this sub-total is not impressive you must be sure you have correctly and fully captured pertinent costs in operations for the current situation and the future 'fixed' situation. If this apparent 'savings' amount is not impressive perhaps the problem was not a great or the cure is not as necessary. Perhaps the cure is not as effective. Perhaps it might be the wrong cure.

## **Examples of Hard Costs**

- technology hardware such as computers, servers, field gear
- technology communications equipment such as routers, cables, 'bandwidth'
- technology software such as operating systems, off-the-shelf applications, custom coded applications, fixed services to customize or configure such software
- ongoing support and maintenance costs for hardware and software
- labour, supervision and overheads for the operations of technology and processes, in current state
- any employees added because of new processes caused by the proposed project, priced at fully loaded wage rates
- building extensions, vehicles, tools, furniture and many other 'hard goods'
- new data which is bought, leased or accessed on subscription
- data entry and verification such as inventory lists, asset locations, vehicle or work records which are part of the software conversion and triggered by the project
- back-up and like systems
- storage devices and associated costs
- web specific hardware and communication assets
- project closure celebrations and related team rewards
- advertising and cost of sales expenses associated with revenue generation
- data centre, equipment room and other required construction
- internet installations and ASP hosting costs
- and more that only you know about

**<u>Examples of Soft Costs</u>**

- training and change management time that is part of and triggered by the project
- interest charges and taxes when applicable and worth including
- increases to insurance or legal fees associated directly with the project
- data modeling, testing and pilot costs
- development of Service Level Agreements and other contract negotiation time
- administration and project, program or portfolio management
- travel and communication costs attributable to the subject
- salaries including loading factors for vacation, pension, space, desks, supplies
- printing and office supplies
- prorated expenses attributable to the project
- consulting and legal fees
- project plan prep and project management training
- insurance and allowances for liabilities
- web specific application design and/or software
- and more that only you know about

## Savings, Revenues and Benefits

Remember, you have to build a full matrix of operational and other savings, revenues or other benefits by activity by volume by department which is applicable to identifying those that will change or become possible as a result of this proposed project which delivers new and continuing operational effects on the transactions of the enterprise.

## Examples of Hard Savings

- the lessening, cancellation or deferral of any of the above hard costs either by volume or pricing
- the interest on the capital deferment or cancellation of purchases for new infrastructure etc.
- the loss of employees at fully loaded wages, who are no longer needed in their previous roles, whether they actually leave the firm or are reassigned
- the differences in labour volumes, labour rates, overtime, supervision and overheads for the operations of technology and processes, in the new state vs. the old current/past state
- and more that only you know about

## Examples of Soft Savings

- any lessening or deferral of any of the above soft costs either by volume or price
- where vehicle maintenance and fuel costs are lessened due to improved routing or less field visits
- taxes on labour expenses saved
- management and supervision of saved labour services
- some overhead of buildings, equipment and services on saved labour
- where interest costs are lessened as a result of less need for borrowed funds
- where parts and supplies last longer due to improved supplier management
- and more that only you know about

## Examples of Revenues and Monetary Benefits

- Increased revenues from selling *more products and services* to existing clients
- Increased revenues from selling existing products and services to *new clients*
- Increased revenues from selling *new products or services* to existing or new clients
- The interest 'earned' or not spent on bank loans due to a new ability to collect revenues sooner
- Revenues actually realized instead of written off as 'bad debt' losses
- and more that only you know about

## Process Improvements: derived savings and valued:

- where a labour (time and salary) function is replaced and is no longer needed
- where a labour function is made quicker: i.e. less time, labour and salary is charged
- or the inverse where more units of work are done for the same labour cost or in the same time
- where a labour function is more effective: i.e. less errors, less do-overs, less backlog
- where a labour function is made more straightforward (easier) and so is transferred to employees of lower pay grades so gross payroll costs are less
- where a customer self serve access replaces or reduces an employee labour service
- where an automated function replaces a labour function
- when taxes on labour expenses saved are also saved
- when insurance fees or liability savings due to factual information being available to employees and/or customers (directly) are created

- where parts last longer or are replaced more easily due to improved controls on internal repairs or inventories
- where interest costs are lower due to more rapid inventory churn or simply less inventory on hand
- where services are simply provided faster for customers
- and more that only you know about

## Examples of Assigned or Imputed Cost or Benefit Values

- representing certain broad cost/revenue predictions and enterprise value creation
- expected increases in overall revenues or decreases on overall costs at the group, department or divisional level where specifics are not able to be determined
- expected increases in overall efficiencies of a group, department or divisional staff
- expected effectiveness that creates an embedded strength or value in the organization and which can be categorized in terms of dollars or percentages of known dollars
- expected lessening of risk of legal action, taxes, penalties or other such 'levies' that can be categorized in dollars or percentages of known dollars
- expected savings or revenues derived from more successful collection of invoiced and/or overdue accounts
- and so much more that only you know about

# BUSINESS CASES IN NINE EASY STEPS

Generally when presenters speak, when authors write and even when politicians or clergy deliver meaningful public messages they follow another variation of the 'rule of three'.

1. First: they introduce you briefly to what they are about to tell you.
2. Second: they tell you at sufficient length and detail what it was they actually intended to tell you.
3. Third: they repeat a summary of what they just told you.

This way you optimize one's ability to hear, to listen and eventually to understand. Sometimes this rule is applicable when trying to communicate with teenagers.

We suggest that you keep this rule of three concepts in mind as you work through any business case as outlined below in nine parts. Don't just repeat something three times; instead share your wisdom with your audience in three waves: brief intro, full details and summary wrap-up. Our straightforward nine part model is offered below.

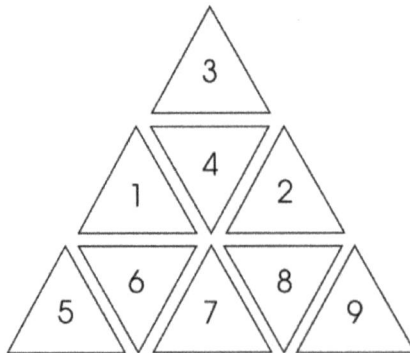

Even though the Pitch, below, is numbered as ONE (1) we probably can't start writing it until steps Three (3) and Four (4) are underway because you need some sense of the problem and its effects before you write anything. Ditto for step TWO (2), the Executive Summary. So that is why the pyramid is topped by 3, supported by 4 before the side steps of 1 and 2 are begun. Both 1 and 2 are updated, shaped and smoothed as each step's narrative improves, they likely never get actually final until after the project starts or perhaps after it completes. The Pitch is number 1 because it is the most critical, every day in every meeting, encounter or presentation.

## The Elevator Pitch, the Current Situation and Executive Summary

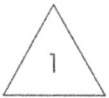 **The 'Elevator Pitch' and Its Rapid Fire Delivery**

A 20-40 word 15-25 second summary of the problem, the pain and the likely cure formulated up front to share with eventual stakeholders that sets out an initial scope for your business case narrative.

How do you describe the situation briefly, accurately, truthfully with confidence and really quickly? Can you do it in an elevator between 5 floors (yours and the CEOs) during a chance 20 second encounter? You must be prepared to do so. As commented March 18, 2013 in a Hubspot.com blog by Marta Kagan, "A closer look at some of (Steve) Jobs' most famous keynotes reads like a presentation in 'headlines': *powerful, memorable, specific statements that consistently add up to fewer than 140 characters*". A Twitter ready elevator pitch; can you imagine?

Some people prefer to start with an elevator pitch, the 20-40 word brief description of the problem and its importance to being solved. This is a most critical succinct statement to make if you are caught in the elevator or in the coffee line with the senior boss, the big shooter, who asks you what you are working on. The future of your business case and your project will depend on the caliber of your pitch, even if you never say it on an elevator. You must write this super short story first for three reasons:

1. If you can't summarize how the situation creates a real risk or failure or missed opportunity, with seriousness and a sense of potential solutions on the spot, whenever and wherever asked, you will never be able to defend your case. If you ever get it written.
2. This pitch is the core from which all research and writing effort follows because this is the simplest basic outline of your project focus that you must constantly come back to.
3. It is your first statement of project scope as well as its urgency and its potential payback.

This pitch may in fact be the moment in your current assignment when the boss really cares about you and your contribution to the organization, so you must be fully prepared to quickly and powerfully fire back with your best 15 second pitch.

The pitch is a summary used as a frame of reference, the essential beginning of your project scope, the reference frame for all your upcoming research and documentation. The pitch becomes the core of your Executive Summary but it lives on as your best short stand-alone statement. Just like the spark of a forest fire, your pitch will grow outward in a number of directions, sometimes with energy and wind at your back and sometimes with wind forces directly in front of you.

You will always need to be aware of what you are fighting for, so you need a really brief statement of mission purpose, scope and expectation. It is very likely that your elevator pitch will evolve and grow better (but not longer) over time. You must always keep it short and at the ready. For GIS themes frame the matter in its geospatial or location based aspect.

Remember that the early pitch cannot have any ROI measures or real timelines because you are at the very front end of the concept. As you near the final prep of your case document you will have approximate and useful financial measures, timeframes and resource requirements. Even these will not be 'best' until the project manager you engage actually draws out the inputs, the steps, the outcomes and the resources will you have an opportunity to speak to ROI and NPV. And even then, as you know, you avoid decimals and you frame expectations in ranges of values.

A good storyteller always places his tale in an imaginable familiar place. The audience must feel comfortable. If it is a project about vehicles, the audience member should imagine themselves comfortably driving one, even if it is an amazing 18-wheel transport, or a bus, or a snow-plow. If it is a project about demographics and marketing to retail trade areas, the audience must imagine themselves receiving the marketing piece and visiting the store. Credibility and buy-in needs to be achieved.

The pitch is crucial at the beginning of your entire effort because it lives as the core of the whole project. As you work through each section you probably will tighten and perfect the pitch, but it is always your core, your scope.

Some examples:

<u>A good and complete but lengthy description:</u>

*e.g. " a GIS based project that uncovers the very high cost this year of managing our fleet of 275 trucks and how a GPS driven application of a Fleet Management System will minimize our fuel expenses and cut some overtime, will optimize our delivery completion rates while we maximize intervals for vehicle maintenance as this will extend vehicle lifetimes significantly by up to 25 percent ".* (64 words spoken in 24-32 seconds)

<u>Or somewhat better:</u>

*e.g. " an application to install a GIS/GPS driven Fleet Management System to minimize today's fuel expenses and cut overtime, to optimize delivery completions while maximizing vehicle maintenance intervals, thus extending the lifetimes of our 275 vehicles significantly, almost 25% "* (38 words spoken is 16-21 seconds)

<u>Or very much better:</u>

*e.g. "a GIS/GPS driven Fleet Management System that minimizes fuel, overtime, delivery failures and optimizes fleet maintenance that extends our 275 vehicle lifetime a significant 20-25 percent".* (26 words spoken in 14-18 seconds)

Short, but still about 189 characters. Can you trim this to 140 for Twitter?

<u>Or the one floor one stop Twitter ready elevator ride version:</u>

*e.g. "a GIS fleet system that lowers costs and extends truck life"* (11 words spoken in no time at all) (64 Twitter ready characters) and always say enthusiastically before the executive leaves your chance encounter : " **and it's really exciting**!"

Just look at the high number of very powerful executive grabbing words in each version. Look at how each shorter version holds on to the most critical points to grab attention. Note that the essential message of the first example is not diminished at all in the shorter 38 or 26 word versions which are shorter, more quickly stated and yet just as effective. The 11 word pitch will still get the executive's attention because lower costs and longer life are very powerful outcomes. He will surely invite you to a meeting to elaborate. So be ready, always be ready. **ALWAYS**!

Can you find or write a 50 word pitch about a favorite project of yours? Can you rewrite two or three shorter versions? Can you create a powerful one-stop version? Go head then. Try it.

Even when you have expanded the elevator pitch into becoming your one page executive summary, using key sentences from all other seven active sections, the updated pitch itself, perhaps the Twitter sized one, becomes the succinct word title of your agenda items and presentations.

## The Executive Summary

The Executive Summary is written last because only then do you know what to say, only then have you expanded your pitch by taking key text from every section, in order, throughout your now 40-50 page narrative.

The executive summary becomes the one page extended pitch because your original really short elevator pitch now has supporting evidence to present, to explain, to justify.

In fact you actually write the Executive Summary only after you have completed your research, evaluation and chosen the recommended action. Only then can you see the whole picture for yourself. Only then can you be effective in summarizing all that work, all those words, for the senior management and other key readers. Only then can you include financials and resource levels, time blocks and defined outcomes.

The actual Executive Summary, the one page that you expect the executives to actually read, is written after all else. That is so you can summarize everything that you now know and have included in the other nine sections of the business case. This Executive Summary is placed at the front of the document. It over-writes or consumes the elevator pitch that often becomes the attention getting opening and compelling first sentence of the full written document.

Commonly one would copy and paste the most compelling text from throughout the narrative that follows in the remaining eight to nine sections (described below), then fix the grammar and language flow, delete the many extra words in order to derive ONE PAGE of summary, which all executives are expected to read, and most actually will.

Never exceed two face pages, one paper sheet, with your Executive Summary! **NEVER**!

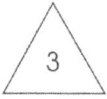

# The Current Situation: Problem Statement and/or Opportunity Description

This is a well told story describing in some detail the current situation in which a problem or opportunity has been identified and an IT/GIS cure is anticipated

This section includes details of why the current situation is a problem. It speaks to who and what processes are affected and which costs, penalties, service levels and even reputations are in trouble because of this problem or missed opportunity. It alerts the reader to the magnitude of the issue and therefore hints that a solution of some size and seriousness may be required.

- Describe the problem or the opportunity being addressed and why its time is now.
- Point out how the GIS and IT applications are involved today, or could be and/or why they are not yet.
- Qualitative: be strategic, tactical, brief, critical and compelling.
- Quantitative: use known direct measured outcomes of the issue where possible and explain clearly when assigned values are used and who is the expert owner of these values
- Do not write in a speculative fashion. Use researched statistics, not speculative ones
- If you do not have enough data or accurate enough data say so, say why and offer a timeline to add such data even though you may be prepared as the sole expert to suggest how negative the data will prove to be when included
- Describe WHY this situation is harmful to the business unit, division or enterprise.
- Describe who in senior management is the reluctant owner of the problem, who is the happy owner of the solution and who are the collective owners of the resulting prosperity
- Relate to the organization's mission and vision where possible

- Avoid 'the world will end' statements of doom;
  - o be factual yet optimistic that eventually you will recommend solutions

## Current Costs; Rationale for Action; Benefits of Top Three Options

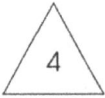

## 4 Effects, Costs and Risks Resulting from the Current Situation

In this section we determine the service, financial and image costs that the current situation is triggering. The penalties incurred today.

The objective of this section is obviously to make clear in each stakeholder's mind that the current situation is not acceptable for the medium and long term even if it is tolerable or 'manageable' in the near term. The fact that the current situation in itself has caused the awareness of the problem and the researched writing of a preliminary business case is validation that something should be done in time. As often quoted in politics and senior management mission statements: the status quo is not a viable option.

Relate all effects, costs and corporate risks that currently result from the current situation, the problem or the opportunity not yet met. Risks here speak to those which the corporation endures because of today's operational problem, state or status quo. Relate risks to the company's ability to grow, its efficiency of overall functioning or its competitive rank in its market. Projects risks are different and can be mentioned but they are not triggers for approving or denying a project. These risks are factors to manage within the project or to fund as contingencies or corrective costs once the project is launched.

Discuss quantitative matters such as money spent, revenue lost or undue risks, liabilities, reworks, throw-aways and employee turnover borne by the current situation, the status quo. Also deal with qualitative outcomes that today may relate to diminished past values or delayed new values unable to be obtained currently.

In addition to simple cost or expense savings, there may be some higher level strategic or reputation issues surrounding the current challenges such as environmental waste or high energy usage from I&T infrastructure. 'Green I&T' is all the rage in some circles today and can generate strong support for some I&T projects and certainly the use of GIS often arises. But be sure your current issues are truly and significantly non-green before you try to add colour to your story.

While this section should be thorough, keep in mind that any current negatives discussed will directly require corrective measures in the solutions of steps six and seven. So if you aren't going to solve it tomorrow with your proposal, don't emphasize it as a bad thing today. However, if it is ethically correct to mention it now, then it remains ethically correct to mention its continuance even with your proposed options. Keep in mind too that nothing builds respect in your work better than being ethical and thorough as long as you keep the balance.

## 5. Rationale for Exploiting the Opportunity or Correcting the Problem

This speaks to why action will be necessary or valuable and speaks to corporate image and risk mitigation, service levels and growth indicators, cost management and KPIs.

This is the time when you write about the importance of solving this problem or taking advantage of the identified opportunity that has arisen. Solving problems is usually fairly straightforward as there will be errors to avoid, costs to stop or minimize, revenues to increase and service levels to make better. In comparison to industry standards, public expectations or regulatory imperatives, the solving of an I&T or business problem should be easy to justify. Frame your case in the geospatial realm of 'where'.

Opportunities are a little different in that there may be more skepticism about the existence of the opportunity or more challenge as to why jump for it, why now, why in this I&T manner. Again competitive pressures may be on side, or public expectation. Shareholder interest and Board of Directors' desire for progress may play well here as might public perceptions or even politics in government. If such opportunities are rare in your industry then that is a positive argument for action. If there are many and varied opportunities popping up every year the challenge of selling your project may lose some attractiveness.

Solving problems is always considered a good thing and taking advantage of uncommon opportunities is what sets great enterprises apart from ordinary ones. Here is your chance to determine if a location based I&T Business Case for change is timely.

Corporate Social Responsibility or CSR themes are well suited to more green I&T, the consumption of less energy and that impact on the environment. As such your business case may be a worthy candidate for a CSR initiative. Be sure that you can isolate the extra savings and/or the extra costs of your green versus non-green options so that decision makers can understand the implications

This is an interesting section of the case because if you are still grasping at rationale for action, or reaction, then either your sense of urgency is early or your pitch did not get the attention it should. This section is not a first alert to your audience because by now you should have done that admirably. This section is to add evidence and strategic mission based frameworks to the concept to cement its acceptance. One never wants your Reviewers or the decision board to still wonder about the problem when they should be weighing the solutions.

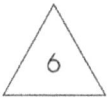

## Top Three Options for Consideration

6    Here we identify and describe the top three options, the *only three* presentable options.

Ah yes: The power of three! Common in most business planning and strategic thinking is to settle on the best three distinctive options. This is partly because discussing any more than three becomes too complicated. This is more because there really are only three core choices: don't do it; do some of it; and do it all. Any other choice is merely a variation or interpretation of the big three. For example even the 1960s classic movie *The Good, The Bad and The Ugly* avoided more variations than three by not adding the really good, the somewhat bad and the very ugly. Three was enough to make the point of one strong hero to endorse, one likeable scoundrel to tolerate if necessary and one nasty gunslinger to reject.

This is not a long section of the case document. The goal here is to describe the three decision choices in terms of the nature of their activities, the changes they would bring and the outputs they would create. This section is not a detailed breakdown of each choice, merely an explanation of the type of choice. Details and a sense of ranked values and outcomes is in the next section.

So no matter what, do not exceed three choices for your stakeholders to review and for your decision makers to choose from. The decision will be hard enough without adding unnecessary choices after the basic three.

Plan A: Hold to Status Quo by deciding after deliberation to do nothing for now.

- Explain briefly what this option implies, what outputs continue and why this option remains valid.
- Be objective and deliver factual and expert driven information that describes the implications (not the merits) of maintaining the current operational process
- Do not explain here why this choice was or was not chosen; that is the next section
- Describe the effects, the positive and negative impacts of doing nothing *at this time*.
- Use costs and service challenges to explain what staying the course means
- Use cautionary text and project costs, identify risks that create a sense of the lesser attractiveness of this do-nothing decision.
- A conscious fact based decision to 'do nothing' can be a respectable management decision as long as all factors about costs, risks, and benefits are known and understood.

Plan B: Do something partial to accommodate being cheaper or faster or temporary.

- Plan B here is a full solution to only part of the problem and not a part solution to the entire problem.
  - There is a really critical difference here. Be alert to the distinctions.

- Discuss clearly which actions are completed and which ones are postponed
- Describe the effects, the positive and negative impacts of attacking some but not all of the issues that matter
- Use high level costs and benefits to explain how some overall benefit will accrue from doing something, from doing the listed portions.
- Leave the 'final balance' sense of this plan being good, or even good enough, but imply if this in fact may not be a wise decision, not a strategic or tactical benefit to the enterprise.
- Do not compare the merits of this option versus the other two options in this section, that is for the next one
- Use balanced text regarding the trade-off of costs vs. revenue, risks vs. growth, progress vs. mere catch-up to create a resigned acceptance of an OK plan to deal with some but not all of the problems.
- A conscious fact based decision to only go part way, half the distance so to speak, can be a respectable management decision as long as all key factors about costs, risks, and benefits are known.
- Everyone must understand this is only part way. It is a plan to complete one aspect in full to solve one part of the problem. This approach is not approving simply doing part of the full job and hanging there until something else happens or is decided.
- There is an obligation to explain *why not settle all of it* or *why the half measure and delay* to those stakeholders who may be predisposed to expect a more complete response to a matter of such importance to them or the firm. Your case narrative must deal with the *why not all* and *why not in one package* conundrum.

Plan C: The most often optimal plan to maximize the beneficial outcome:

- Discuss how the full solution satisfies the corporate goals and fixes the majority of the full problem
- Explain well, make it obvious.

- Describe the positive impacts of getting this problem dealt with now, and not bearing the negatives of continuing with the status quo or a compromise solution
- Use revenues, key performance indicators, savings, service improvements and any other positive improvements that directly and even indirectly flow from the completion of this full bodied plan
- Use action and service oriented text that creates a sense of success
- A firm decision to settle this matter fully over time is also a valid quality management decision.
- Planned phases and planned increments to the project effort are often used to support the full plan. Explain how doing so with two to three major checkpoints along the way is good management. Explain how funding and resources, scope and expectations can be renewed at each phase start through the benefit of the then current facts.
- This is not the same as Plan B which designs a project of limited scope with no plan for phased continuance. This is a full intent to complete the whole project in phases and with decision confirmation points planned, dated and budgeted now, in advance. Emphasis on budgeted now in advance.

Usually the recommended choice will be discussed third, last. This is because the document is a flow of the story. You are setting the stage for the next chapter and the one after that. So as your reader walks through your case he will be forming his own opinion of the merits of each option. By discussing the lesser options first your reader would probably share your views that these two options are not optimal, that each of them has at least one serious flaw. Then your reader comes to the third option and as predicted sees that the flaws in the other options have been dealt with or did nod not occur at all. The third and best option may still have a few minor flaws because business activities usually identify or create them. In light of the 80/20 approach some applications sought by some stakeholders may still not get funded.

This third and preferred option has less flaws or has them under better management control. At this point, for his own reasons as well as those written, your reader would likely here be aligned with your third option. It will be clearly obvious. Compelling.

## Weighing Options; the Recommendation and Resource needs

### Returns Values and Impacts of Each Option

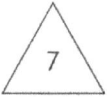

Each option is detailed in terms of costs, benefits, regulations, risks, methods, resources, timing, market support to generate Returns and values. Explain each option's strategic significance with a slight emphasis on the Impact the stronger option may have on employees, customers and other stakeholders

This section gets into the real details of all your research into the financial, near-financial and non-financial aspects of the three optional solutions for the current problem or opportunity presented in Section 3 of your case report. Recall your three options are comparable to your personal options if your car is old, suffering, out of service sometimes and well beyond the warranty period. You can keep it running as best possible with fairly constant repairs along with applications that now fail to function OR you can buy a used car that is much better that holding on to an end-of-life auto but is lacking the latest tools OR you can buy a new car with a full warranty and many new applications that your old car simply never had. The I&T business case is not really much different, just more expensive and more complicated.

Expand in detail on each optional plan with full description of each plan's actions and outcomes along with costs and benefits, directly and indirectly. This section serves to confirm to the reader what was sensed in the section above, that two options really don't make sense. Even if they are viable, there is available proof as to why each of the two secondary choices are clearly not recommended, as they are too risky or too sub-optimal. After digesting the power of the recommended plan and the described rationale, the reader could in fact defend this choice to a non-reader, or argue its merits to a reader who doubts the suggested plan. When that actually happens, your document has become bullet-proof.

**Status quo acceptance**: or the decision that keeping things as they are can be an acceptable and manageable choice. This is where your decision makers would proactively, objectively and consciously decide to do nothing; more probably almost nothing. However, from an I&T or GIS application sense, no project would be launched and no funding would be required... at this time.

This is somewhat like the 10% solution because it may be that your research revealed a real major issue that simply must be corrected but along with a task of building new capacity or new capability. For example you find ongoing crashes of your non-supported Windows 3.1 that trigger an unavoidable upgrade to current Windows 7 and associated hardware. This is like finding out the roof is falling in and while a new building is not desirable or necessary at this time, a warm dry work area is mandatory.

In this option the writer must clearly describe the costs of enduring the current situation, the risks that carry on and any missed benefits or strategic penalties that might happen. Only if the costs and risks are delineated can the approvers compare this option to the other two on a basis of the returns, the values and the impacts of each option.

There is an obligation to explain what would drive a recommendation of *why not* or *why not now* to stakeholders who may have been expecting some action.

**Optional or partial plan**: the one which appears to solve the key problems but does not seek to overly change the process, the system or the current outcomes. This option is the compromise that overcomes perhaps 30-40% of the problems, the really obvious and public ones, by implementing some fixes. It does not fully overcome the majority of problems not does it build a platform for further growth. It corrects the past perhaps but does not prepare for a future. In the 30% or so solution it is sufficiently corrective and much ahead of 'do nothing' that it has a material benefit that executives may consider a worthwhile 'bang for the buck' even though most of the [problem remains unaddressed.

The 30% plus decision is a classic trade-off. The writer needs to identify the numbers and speak to their credibility as in all parts of the case. There should be no doubt about this choice, which is perfectly viable and often chosen, being merely a partial fix, a compromise of issue over time against money and value. It is a short term tactic not out of step with strategy (pardon the double negative). It is not a strategic step aligned with key corporate goals and missions in most cases. The writer needs to very clear if acceptance of this partial choice also implies if a phase two or three or even four will be needed and if so when.

If the mood of the organization is to go for a 60-70% solution this may be a call for some really deep thinking and open discussion. It all likelihood such a significant effort and investment, without finishing the whole recommended project, may end up being a bad compromise, saving only pennies on costs but missing many dollars of benefits. Maybe not, but the business case writer and key defender needs to be aware of this possibility and be prepared to ignite a lively discussion so that whatever the final executive decision is, it is not a set-up for aggravation and regret later on. Beware of unintended consequences.

This partial option needs to also explain why waiting is sub-optimal and what cost or penalties stay on by only solving part of the problem, acting on part of the opportunity.

**Optimal and likely most desirable plan**. This third and final option involves factual numbers and descriptions that identify added insight and emphasis on the beneficial outcomes for the overall health or success of the firm; alignment with goals and performance measures, mission and vision strategies including CSR. At this point the reader should strongly sense, on their own, the preferred plan and why it is optimal.

This section may not be the longest but it must be the strongest. You will restate the simple succinct power of your Elevator Pitch with those powerful action benefit words except this time you now have numbers, timing and performance based outcomes.

## Recommendation and Rationale

This is where you tell the reader what you indicated you would tell him. This is where the reader gets the hard proof of what he already figured was the best option. You should not begin this part, this chapter until you work through the less optimal choices and both you and the reader have that AHA! moment. That is when readers realize what the preferred choice must be, needs to be, just has to be. So don't write about this preferred choice first or second, but do it third. Write at least 50% more information, more benefits and more strategic mapping to goals in the text of your preferred choice, the last one presented, the one that will be remembered as the reader moves to the next chapter.

Drive home the reasons for the preferred option and why it is preferred over each of the other two at this time. Refer back to your Elevator Pitch for the essence of the recommendation.

This is the conclusion of the comparative section but one expects the audience to already understand why the preferred option is the best one. If this section is still weak it is only because the prior two sections were not clear.

This is where one identifies measurements that may be done after the project to support the outcomes expected.

This is your succinct explanation of WHY the chosen plan is superior and aligned with corporate goals and desirable for reasons of service, revenue, regulation and strategic direction. Write in some detail covering perhaps seven to ten aspects of the overall superiority of this chosen plan. Include brief explanations in one or two lines on the two to three most important points as to why the rejected plans were not prudent supportable decisions. While selling the chosen plan question up to three features about the alternatives.

Describe how this project contributes to the overall capacity and capability of the firm, those two assets that generate success. Describe the story about the new state and how this is desirable, effective and efficient for the firm. Then ….Ask for approval, here and now.

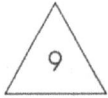

## Project Outline and Resource Expectations

Before any committee or person will approve and fund your project you must outline a general schedule of project plan and a sense of resources, money and people that will be needed when and to do what.

This is not a project level plan but a calendar level outline of what to expect and what needs to be planned in detail following approval to proceed. A full list of every contributor to the case document is necessary. An appendix of a reasonable number of tables, charts, lists and graphics may follow the nine key parts. A bibliography of sources and quotation acknowledgements should also follow.

This appendix may be unique to your organization for how you present and approve project business cases by answering such protocols as: what happens next, who will do what and when over the next few months.

Your practice should include at least a general calendar of events that demonstrate not only the probable flow of work by quarter or year end, resource requirements and expenditures. Most importantly this section demonstrates that you, the author, have all these matters well in hand.

Dates should be milestone dates such as one month, one quarter and one year from a hypothetical 'start date' as opposed to naming months such as September, January and May. This is because milestones that matter will depend on the day/ month of project and funding approval.

All this falls into more detailed place after the executive approval of the case and the project. Each organization deals with these matters differently.

This may be a good place for you to insert your version of the <u>General Cost Breakdown Summary</u> as described further in the next section of this guidebook.

## Appendices for Tables, References and Supporting Data

- This section is the backup for all that is above. Do not expect most readers to bother with this section, especially if your narrative and support is compelling.
- Generally, those who trust you and align with your case will trust your case conclusions. They will expect fully that you have plenty of backup and supporting evidence even though they do not need to see it.
- However, every executive team has a "numbers geek"; so understand and expect that at least one person will read this section in detail and will probably be looking for errors or omissions. Be prepared, be bullet-proof.

The best way to start is simply to start. Take nine sheets of paper and title them according to our model. Write down in point form any and all ideas, questions and key points you want to make in each step. Go do more research and speak with stakeholders everywhere. Write down the points they make or modify yours if they add strength to your earlier thoughts.

Turn the points into sentences, fix the grammar, adjust the spacing and attend to the spelling. By now you are 2/3 done. Just keep going until you are satisfied. The write your Executive Summary.

# THE GENERAL COST BREAKDOWN SUMMARY

One of the awkward issues in writing (and reading) a successful business case relates to the use of resources (money and people) and the breakdown of their use. Usually a worthy I&T project can cost hundreds of thousands of dollars or even millions. When the executive summary is read by decision makers they typically see the total amount and only sometimes see a two-to-five year schedule of budget sub-totals. This can be frustrating to those who enjoy deep details. They might feel like shooting at your case document. Of course some buy into the project costs, but shouldn't, in the absence of enough or satisfactory basic detail.

The key breakdown should identify how much is being spent on what activity or input, what share of the total is this and what happens to the overall total if up to three of the big items end up far off expectation, what if an entry is too low or too high. Recall our Contingency versus Sensitivity discussion above.

One effective way to satisfy the need for some enlightenment on costs is to use our General Breakdown Summary. In this table we take care to use a maximum of ten divisions or topics. We are only trying to add some high level 'orders of magnitude' information for major cost categories or sets of resources. Decision makers must see enough detail to be comfortable in the proposal as written and in the ability of the case writer to fully understand all aspects at that time. Nine or ten topics will always be enough to capture all sub-totals while still being able to identify the key ones, the big ones, the real targets.

In other words answer the "what if" objection before anyone in decision mode can affect the presentation of the case. Demonstrate your sensitivity about the analysis of the big two, three or four really major project components. Remember, this is the business case stage, not the detailed plan stage, not the detailed engineering stage. Remember that all values are preliminary at this point anyway. So again, ten breakdowns are plenty, and it's the few hugely sensitive ones that warrant variable analysis. Yes you can do them all, but small minor categories even 50% or 90% off rarely impact the total case.

Here is an example of a completed General Cost Breakdown Summary:

Note the use of Sensitivity in the columns for some key factors and the line for Contingency.

Note that no decimals are used and all monies are in 000's. This is a scale of magnitude display to demonstrate relative share of overall budget levels in general.

| Typical Major Project Components | Budget(000) | Percent share of total project | Plus 15% Sensitivity on top 3 components | Minus 8% Sensitivity on top 3 components |
|---|---|---|---|---|
| Needs Assessment | $195 | 6% | | |
| Software | $390 | 12% | $448 | $359 |
| Hardware | $260 | 8% | | |
| Project Management | $162 | 5% | | |
| System Integration | $195 | 6% | | |
| Contract Staff Augmentation | $292 | 9% | | |
| Data Error Correction | $455 | 14% | $523 | $419 |
| Process Changes | $617 | 19% | $710 | $568 |
| Testing | $130 | 4% | | |
| Training | $227 | 7% | | |
| Sub-Totals | $2925 | 90% | $3143 | $2808 |
| Contingency (10%) | $292 | 10% | $314 | $280 |
| TOTALS | $3,217 | 100% | $3457 or+ 7.5% overall | $3088 or - 4% overall |

**Take Note:**     For your project, make a quick educated guess of how the total costs may break down using the Cost Breakdown Summary approach. The insight you are looking for is not how accurate your cost expectations may be, it is the relative weight that some costs may have versus others. In other words can you see even this early with little or no research and details which of the costs categories will require sensitivity alternatives and which will not?

# THE DEMYSTIFIED  I&T or GIS BUSINESS CASE COMPANION FINANCIAL WORKBOOK

Below we address what we think would be a set of really useful worksheets in an MS Excel or similar workbook to hold your data and make calculations for your project. You may be required to use standard corporate templates or you may be XL literate, able to design your own spreadsheets and workbooks. If not, you will be able to order a functioning set of worksheets from us entitled: "The Demystified I&T GIS Business Case Companion Financial Workbook" on our site ReturnsValuesImpacts.com

We use a set of EIGHT active worksheets. Each worksheet has a dedicated purpose, and each is to be completed by YOU, the business case author, chief proposal defender and star presenter. The "Returns" summary which includes pro forma ROI, NPV and PB is then managed by you as a key part of your case document. Entries on monetary worksheets automatically flow to the ROI and NPV. The first two sheets are samples to let you adjust some entries, to play, on your own to see the resultant changes in ROI and NPV. The final sheet looks to the environmental and CSR trends that are emerging in I/T and GIS.

The worksheets in our companion set are named as:

**ROI Sample**: this is suggested so that the writer and the whole extended team can better understand ROI and how changes to any variable will change the outcome. This is a fairly simple sheet and is intuitive to anyone using it even though just looking at it may not be as powerful as changing some numbers, as one would do with a sensitivity.

**NPV Sample**: this too is suggested so that the writer and the whole extended team can better understand NPV or with a particular interest rate in mind an IRR taking the NPV to zero. Again, how changes to any variable will change the outcome is interesting.

**Project Costs**: as the name implies the writer would canvass all contributors to determine the today costs of all purchases, activities, assets and overheads under that the project is expected to incur during the proposed project period, usually 1 to 5 years. As you can see it can be a good tactic to list cost item names that are not necessarily planned, yet, that will be zero. This is wise because it forces you to check and be sure that zero is the correct answer. Better still it tells your audience that yes you did think of everything and no there are no such costs, this time. Templates are helpful this way because you always get a bigger awareness than if you simply entered only known items. Always enter a zero, do not leave a cell blank or empty. You and your audiences want to be sure that the value is deliberate and not overlooked or missing.

**Benefits and Revenues:** these benefits will be positioned as money even if they tend to be more like operational qualitative values and impacts. Any describable and distinguishable improvement, cancellation or upgrade of monetary benefit to the organization should be captured here or assigned based on internal or external expertise.

**Process Efficiencies:** By definition efficiencies can be expressed in monetary terms while the benefits of such efficiencies might also be described in your narrative as effectiveness: and vice versa. Again this sheet captures monetary values of benefits derived from doing things faster or cheaper or better or with less errors or not at all.

**Savings:** This is straightforward but is left for monetary expenses that are accomplished using less money. Savings in materials, time, headcount, interest, lawsuits, penalties, overtime and price based advantages from discounts or volume.

**ROI and NPV Calculator**: This sheet automatically carries the totals by category from monetary totals of the last four sheets covering Project Costs, Benefits and Revenues, Process Efficiencies and Savings.

**Environmental Impact**: Green aspects and values. Optional for now but as the world grows more sensitive, more cases will need to state the environmental impact or cost of this project being completed as proposed. CSR or Corporate Social Responsibility is not going to go away.

# Time to Get Started

Your next task is to write a business case for GIS or any other branch of I&T; to write a highly effective case story; to write a defensible case and to make it as bullet-proof as you can. May the ideas flow easily, may the reviewers be courteous and may the approvals be enthusiastic.

 Thanks for reading! Why not send me your next elevator pitch?

## About the Author

Greg Duffy has over 25 years of experience at the crossroads of customer service, business operations and information technology in utilities, governments and businesses. He has worked with clients and customers of clients in North America and the Middle East.

He has written many Executive Briefs in true white paper style and been published in IT and GIS oriented journals and magazines. He has spoken at conferences and business education events in Canada, United States, United Arab Emirates and Bahrain to audiences of a few to hundreds. He is a candid and sincere speaker using humour to good effect.

His career experiences have spanned a broad spectrum of IT and GIS based service and product oriented themes such as call centers, marketing, business development, product development, operations, policy and senior management while leading teams of a few to a hundred.

He believes strongly in lifelong learning and the pursuit of curiosity. As such, he always looks forward to a new experience and helping new friends meet new challenges. He earned his Executive MBA mid-career at the University of Toronto's Rotman School of Management.

*Feedback is always welcome. Please pass on any complaints, compliments or suggestions about writing I&T and GIS business cases or about this guide so that we may keep it useful for our readers. Our email is:    greg@ReturnsValuesImpacts.com.*

*Watch www.ReturnsValuesImpacts.com for our next books expected to be available in late 2013.*

*"How Mature is Your GIS? ...How do you know?"*

# Executive Briefs and White Papers by Greg Duffy

CRM and GIS are Paradigms (2009)

G.I. Strategies (2010)

GIS as a Paradigm for *HOW* Municipalities Work (2004)

How Mature is Your GIS? (2010)

IT Portfolio Office Provides a Roadmap for Asset Management and More (2011)

KAPA: - Knowledge At the Point of Action - is the Real Mission for IT (2010)

P.O.S.I.T. from Woodfield: the **P**roject **O**utline **S**cope for **I**nformation **T**echnology (2007)

ROI in Other Words (2005)

ROI Revisited (2005)

The Essence of a Governance Framework for the IT Portfolio (2010)

The Four Streams of IT Programs (2005)

The IT Impact Model applied to Market Segmentation Systems (2010)

Whatever Happened to the 'I' in 'I/T' ? (2005)